GERMAN
IN YOUR
POCKET

A Headway phrasebook

Paul Stocker

Headway · Hodder & Stoughton

British Library Cataloguing in Publication Data

CIP catalogue record for this book is available from the British Libr

ISBN 0 340 50914 7

First published 1990

© 1990 Paul Stocker

Typeset by Wearside Tradespools, Fulwell, Sunderland
Printed in Great Britain for the educational publishing division of
Hodder and Stoughton Ltd, Mill Road, Dunton Green, Sevenoaks
Kent by M & A Thomson Litho Ltd, East Kilbride, Scotland.

Contents

Introduction	4
Pronunciation Guide	5
Basic Expressions	6
Arrival and Departure	7
Accommodation	17
Eating Out	33
Entertainment and Sport	49
Health	65
Travel	73
Shopping	97
Services	113
Essential Information	129
Wordlist	137

Introduction

This new phrase book is an essential accessory for travellers of all ages. The main section of the book consists of phrases and sentences listed in a logical order in sections, and organised in a way which will make it easy for you to select the items which will say what YOU want to say.

You should start by familiarising yourself with the **Pronunciation Guide** (page 5) and the **Basic Expressions** (page 6). If you can, practise the phrases you might need beforehand. To help you understand what is being said to you, you will find coloured boxes headed **You may hear** or **You may see** scattered through the book. There is also a **Wordlist** (page 137) of the commonest words, and a section of **Essential Information**.

Grammar

German-speakers will not usually misunderstand you if you make grammatical mistakes – they will in any case be impressed that you are making an effort to use their language. German is a relatively logical language with few exceptions to its rules. Two short explanations may be useful here:

You German has three words for 'you' to our one. You will notice that all are given in the book, where appropriate. Use as follows:
Sie – polite word for 'you', whether one person or a group; use with anyone you don't know well.
du – informal word for 'you', for just one person; use with a friend, relative, child, or animal.
ihr – as for **du**, but for two or more friends.

The and **a** English-speakers often wonder why there are several words for 'the' and 'a' in German; this is because the basic words **der, die, das** (all of which mean 'the'), and **ein, eine** (meaning 'a' or 'an') change their endings according to where they stand in the sentence – rather like 'he' and 'him' or 'they' and 'them' in English.

Gute Reise!

Pronunciation

- The pronunciation of German is very similar to English, and holds few problems for the unwary! Moreover, letters and combinations of letters are always pronounced the same way. The main points to be aware of are as follows:

symbol		German		English
g	as in	gerade	compare with	get
kh		ich		loch
kv		Quantität		black velvet
s		das		say
sh		spielen		ship
ts		Zimmer		vets
y		ja		yes
z		sie		rose
a		kann		man
aa		fahren		far
ai		wenig		aim
e		wenn		men
ee		wir		seem
ew		Kügel		*see below*
i		bitte		tin
I }	*see below*	Eis		I
y }		leider		fly
o		Woche		not
oh		Person		more
oo		umsteigen		room
ow		laufen		how
oy		heute		boy
ur		möchte		burn

- The German letter ß should be pronounced 's'.
- The sound ew (ü) is pronounced as ee, but with the lips rounded as for oo.
- The 'y' symbol is generally used to represent the vowel sound in, for example, 'fly'. The 'I' symbol is used where this might be mispronounced.
- When you see the following letters in written German, they are always pronounced as shown:

$$sch = sh \qquad v = f$$
$$w = v \qquad ä = e \text{ or } ai$$
$$ei = I \qquad ie = ee$$

- Stressed syllables are indicated in bold type.

5

Basic expressions

Yes/No	Ja/Nein *yaa/nyn*
Please/Thank you	Bitte/Danke *bitter/danker*
Excuse me	Entschuldigung *entshooldeegoong*
I don't know	Ich weiß es nicht *ikh vyss ess nikht*
Do you speak English?	Sprechen Sie Englisch? *shprekhen zee ennglish?*
I (don't) understand	Ich verstehe (nicht) *ikh fairshtai-er (nikht)*
Do you understand?	Verstehen Sie? *fairshtai-en zee?*
Could you speak slower?	Können Sie bitte langsamer sprechen? *kurnen zee bitter langsaamer shprekhen?*
Could you repeat that?	Können Sie das bitte wiederholen? *kurnen zee dass bitter veederhohlen?*
What does that mean?	Was bedeutet das? *vas berdoytet das?*
Pardon?	Wie bitte? *vee bitter?*
Could you translate this for me?	Könnten Sie mir das übersetzen? *kurnten zee meer das ewberzetsen?*
Could you write that down?	Können Sie das bitte aufschreiben? *kurnen zee dass bitter owfshryben?*
Can you help me?	Können Sie mir helfen? *kurnen zee meer helfen?*

ARRIVAL AND DEPARTURE

- This section deals with arriving and departing in German-speaking countries. For information on travel (by air, or by public or private transport), see page 73. Taxis and car hire pages 12–13.
- Watch out for the following differences in place names:

Basle	=	Basel
Black Forest	=	Schwarzwald
Cologne	=	Köln
Geneva	=	Genf
Lake Constance	=	Bodensee
Munich	=	München
Nuremburg	=	Nürnberg
Vienna	=	Wien

Names of other towns in German-speaking countries are spelt similarly in both English and German.

Passport control

I'm here on business	Ich bin geschäftlich hier *ikh bin gersheftlikh heer*
We're here on holiday	Wir sind auf Urlaub hier *veer zint owf oorlowp heer*

I'm/we're staying . . .	Ich bleibe/wir bleiben . . . *ikh blyber/veer blyben . . .*
. . . for 2 days	. . . zwei Tage *tsvy taager*
. . . for 1 week/2 weeks	. . . eine Woche/zwei Wochen *yner vokher/tsvy vokhen*
. . . for 1 month/2 months	. . . einen Monat/zwei Monate *ynern Mohnaat/tsvy mohnaater*
. . . till . . .	. . . bis zum . . . *bis tsoom . . .*

● See page 133 for dates

We're going . . .	Wir fahren . . . *veer faaren . . .*
. . . to the Alps	. . . in die Alpen *in dee alpen*
. . . to Austria	. . . nach Österreich *nakh ursterykh*
. . . to the FRG (West Germany)	. . . in die BRD *in dee bai air dai*
. . . to the GDR (East Germany)	. . . in die DDR *in dee dai dai air*
. . . to Switzerland	. . . in die Schweiz *in dee shvyts*

Customs

- Before going through customs, be sure to check on what is permitted. You can pick up leaflets with current allowances at ports and airports. It may be worth carrying receipts with you.
- If you have something to declare, go through the red exit (*Anmeldepflichtige Waren*); otherwise choose the green exit (*Anmeldefreie Waren*).

I've nothing to declare	Ich habe nichts zu verzollen *ikh haaber nikhts tsoo fairtsolen*
Do I have to declare this?	Muß ich das verzollen? *moos ikh das fairtsolen?*
How much do I have to pay?	Wieviel muß ich zahlen? *veefeel moos ikh tsaalen?*

I've got . . .	Ich habe . . . *ikh haaber . . .*
. . . cigarettes	. . . Zigaretten *tsigareten*
. . . cigars	. . . Zigarren *tsigaren*
. . . tobacco	. . . Tabak *tabak*
. . . spirits	. . . Spirituosen *sphiritoo-ohzen*
. . . wine	. . . Wein *vyn*
. . . perfume	. . . Parfüm *parfewm*

Here's the receipt	Hier ist die Quittung *heer ist dee kvittoong*
It's a present	Es ist ein Geschenk *es ist I-n gershenk*

You may hear:

Ihren Paß bitte *eeren pas bitter*	Your passport, please
Wohin fahren Sie? *vohin faaren zee?*	Where are you travelling to?
Wie lange bleiben Sie? *vee langer blyben zee?*	How long are you staying?
Bitte öffnen Sie . . . *bitter urfnen zee . . .*	Please open . . .
Haben Sie etwas zu verzollen? *haaben zee etvas tsoo fairtsollen?*	Do you have anything to declare?
Dies ist zollpflichtig *deez ist tsollpflikhtig*	You must pay duty on this

Here's my ticket	Hier ist meine Fahrkarte *heer ist myner faarkaarter*
My name is . . .	Ich heiße . . . *ikh hysser . . .*
My flight-number is . . .	Meine Flugnummer ist . . . *myner floognoomer ist . . .*
Here's my address	Hier ist meine Adresse *heer ist myner adresser*

You may see:

Abfahrt	Departures
Ankunft	Arrival
Fluggäste/Passagiere	Passengers
Fluglinie	Airline
Gepäckausgabe	Luggage reclaim
Paßkontrolle	Passport control
Zoll	Customs
Zollfreie Waren	Duty-free shop

Luggage

● Airports and railway stations have luggage trolleys
(*Kofferkulis*), for which a small sum is usually
payable.

Where are the luggage trolleys?	Wo sind die Kofferkulis? *voh zint dee koffer-kooliz?*
Where do we collect our luggage?	Wo holen wir unser Gepäck ab? *voh hohlen veer oonzer gerpek ap?*
Where's the information desk?	Wo ist die Auskunft? *voh ist dee owskoonft?*
There's a bag/case missing	Eine Tasche/Ein Koffer fehlt *I-ner tascher/I-n koffer failt*
My luggage hasn't arrived yet	Mein Gepäck ist noch nicht da *myn gerpek ist nokh nikht daa*
I can't find my luggage	Ich finde mein Gepäck nicht *ikh finder myn gerpek nikht*
Has the luggage from the London flight arrived yet?	Ist das Gepäck von dem Flug aus London schon da? *ist das gerpek fon daim floog ows london shohn daa?*
When will my luggage arrive?	Wann kommt mein Gepäck? *van kommt myn gerpek?*
Could you please find out where my luggage is?	Können Sie bitte herausfinden, wo mein Gepäck ist? *kurnen zee bitter herows-finden, voh myn gerpek ist?*
I'm leaving for . . . tomorrow/ in two days' time	Ich fahre morgen/in zwei Tagen nach . . . *ikh faarer morgen/in tsvy taagen nakh . . .*

11

Taxis

- Look for the sign *Taxistand* (taxi rank). It is not usual to hail a taxi.
- Tipping: about 10%.

Where can I get a taxi?	Wo finde ich ein Taxi? *voh finder ikh I-n taxi?*
Please get me a taxi	Bestellen Sie mir bitte ein Taxi *bershtellen zee meer bitter I-n taxi*
Take me to ...	Fahren Sie mich ... *faaren zee mikh ...*
... this address	... zu dieser Adresse *tsoo deezer addresser*
... the station	... zum Bahnhof *tsoom baanhohf*
... the airport	... zum Flughafen *tsoom flooghaafen*
Could you help me with my luggage?	Können Sie mir mit meinem Gepäck helfen? *kurnen zee meer mit mynem gerpek helfen?*
Please stop here	Bitte halten Sie hier *bitter halten zee heer*
Wait for me, please	Bitte warten Sie auf mich *bitter vaarten zee owf mikh*
How much is it?	Was kostet es? *vas kostet es?*
Keep the change	Es stimmt so *es shtimt zoh*
Can you give me a receipt?	Können Sie mir bitte eine Quittung geben? *kurnen zee meer bitter I-ner kvitoong gaiben?*

Car hire

- Look for the sign *Autoverleih* or *Autovermietung*.

I'd like to hire a car	Ich möchte ein Auto mieten *ikh murkhter I-n owtoh meeten*
I'd like a small/medium/large one	Ich möchte ein kleines/ein mittleres/ein grosses *ikh murkter I-n klynes/I-n mitleres/I-n grohses*
I'd like it for ...	Ich möchte es für ... *ikh murkhter es fewr ...*
... a day	... einen Tag *I-nen taag*
... 2 days	... zwei Tage *tsvy taager*
... a week	... eine Woche *I-ner vokher*
What are the tariffs per day/week?	Was sind die Tarife pro Tag/pro Woche? *vas zint dee tareefer proh taag/proh vokher?*
Can I leave the car in ... ?	Kann ich das Auto in ... zurückgeben? *kan ikh das owtoh in ... tsoorewkgaiben?*
I'd like comprehensive insurance	Ich möchte eine Vollkaskoversicherung *ikh murkhter I-ner folkaskoh-fairzikheroong*
How much deposit must I pay?	Wieviel muß ich hinterlegen? *veefeel moos ikh hinterlaigen?*
Here is my driving licence/my passport	Hier ist mein Führerschein/mein Paß *heer ist myn fewrershyn/myn pas*

Departure

Here is my ticket/boarding card	Hier ist meine Fahrkarte/ meine Bordkarte *heer ist myner faarkaarter/ myner bordkaarter*
Can I take this on board?	Kann ich das mit an Bord nehmen? *kan ikh das mit an bord naimen?*
How much must I pay for the excess?	Was muß ich für das Übergewicht zahlen? *vas moos ikh fewr das ewbergervikht tsaalen?*
From which gate does our flight leave?	Von welchem Flugsteig geht unser Flug? *fon velkhem floogshtyg gait oonzer floog?*
Has flight (BA960) been called?	Wurde Flug (BA960) schon aufgerufen? *voorder floog (bai aa noyn zekhs nool) shohn owfgeroofen?*
Why is flight (BA960) delayed?	Warum ist der Flug (BA960) verspätet? *varoom ist dair floog (bai aa noyn zekhs nool) fairshpaitet?*
Can I book a seat on another/ the next flight?	Kann ich einen Platz für einen anderen Flug/den nächsten Flug reservieren? *kan ikh ynen plats fewr ynen anderen floog/dain nekhsten floog rezairveeren?*

You may hear:

Der Flug nach . . . hat . . . Minuten Verspätung *dair floog nakh . . . hat . . . minooten fairshpaitoong*	The flight to . . . will be . . . minutes late

14

Arrival and departure

I've missed my ...	Ich habe ... verpaßt
	ikh haabe ... fairpast
... plane	... meinen Flug ...
	mynen floog
... connection	... meinen Anschluß ...
	mynen anshlooss ...
... coach/bus	... meinen Bus ...
	mynen boos
... train	... meinen Zug ...
	mynen tsoog
... ferry	... meine Fähre ...
	myner fairer

● When looking at timetables on German stations, remember that both departures (*Abfahrt*) and arrivals (*Ankunft*) will be on display.

Which platform does the train to Bonn leave from?	Von welchem Gleis fährt der Zug nach Bonn ab?
	fon velkhem glys fairt dair tsoog nakh bonn ap?
Which are the carriages for ... ?	Welche Wagen fahren nach ... ?
	velkher vaagen faaren nakh ... ?
Here's my reservation	Hier ist meine Reservierung
	heer ist myner rezairveeroong
When does the next train for ... leave?	Wann fährt der nächste Zug nach ... ?
	van fairt dair nekhster tsoog nakh ... ?
Does the train stop in ... ?	Hält der Zug in ... ?
	helt dair tsoog in ... ?
When will the ferry sail?	Wann fährt die Fähre ab?
	van fairt dee fairer ap?
When will the ferry dock?	Wann kommt die Fähre an?
	van komt dee fairer an?

How long is the crossing from . . . to . . . ?	Wie lange dauert die Überfahrt von . . . nach . . . ? *vee langer dowert dee ewberfaart fon . . . nakh . . . ?*
Where is cabin number 3, please?	Wo ist Kabine Nummer drei bitte? *voh ist kabeener noomer dry, bitter?*
Is there a cabin free?	Haben Sie noch Kabinen frei? *haabern nokh kabeenen fry?*

- For making bookings, see page 80.

How far is it?	Wie weit ist es? *vee vyt ist ess?*
Where are the toilets?	Wo sind die Toiletten? *voh zint dee twaletten?*
I've been waiting for 30 minutes	Ich warte seit dreißig Minuten *ikh vaarter zyt drysig minooten*
Where is . . . ?	Wo ist . . . ? *voh ist . . . ?*
. . . the way out	. . . der Ausgang *dair owsgang*
. . . the railway-station	. . . der Bahnhof *dair baanhohf*
. . . the underground (subway) station	. . . die U-Bahnstation *dee oo-baanshtatsyohn*
Where can I change some money?	Wo kann ich Geld wechseln? *voh kan ikh gelt vekhseln?*

- If you have not made a booking before departure, there are several ways of finding a room. Look out for:
  Zimmernachweis or *Zimmervermittlung*: a room-booking service at airports or major stations.
  Fremdenverkehrsbüro or *Fremdenverkehrsamt*: the tourist information office, which offers a similar service.
- *Zimmer frei* will indicate that there are vacancies. *Belegt* or *Besetzt* indicates that all the rooms are taken.
- The choice of accommodation is usually between the following:
  - **Hotel (garni)**   hotel (bed and breakfast)
  - **Gasthaus/Gasthof**   inn
  - **Pension/Fremdenheim**   guest house
  - **Jugendherberge**   youth hostel

17

Booking a room

Do you have an accommodation list?	Haben Sie ein Hotelverzeichnis? *haaben zee I-n hohtelfairtsykhniss?*
Can you reserve a room for me/us?	Können Sie mir/uns ein Zimmer reservieren? *kurnen zee meer/oons I-n tsimmer reserveeren?*
. . . in a hotel	. . . in einem Hotel *in I-nem hohtel*
. . . in a guest house	. . . in einer Pension *in I-ner pentsiohn*
. . . in the town centre	. . . in der Stadtmitte *in dair shtat-miter*
. . . near the airport/station	. . . in der Nähe vom Flughafen/Bahnhof *in dair nai-er fom flooghaafen/baanhohf*
. . . for 1/2 nights	. . . für eine Nacht/zwei Nächte *fewr yner nakht/tsvy nekhter*
I'm not sure yet how long we'll stay	Ich weiß noch nicht, wie lange wir bleiben *ikh vys nokh nikht, vee langer veer blyben*
Do you have anything cheaper/better?	Haben Sie etwas Billigeres/Besseres? *haaben zee etvas biligeres/besseres?*
How do I get there?	Wie komme ich dahin? *vee komer ikh dahin?*
Can you show me on a street-map?	Können Sie es mir auf einem Stadtplan zeigen? *kurnen zee es meer owf I-nem shtat-plan tsygen?*

Accommodation

What does it cost . . . ?	Was kostet es . . . ? *vas kostet es . . . ?*
. . . per night	. . . pro Nacht *proh nakht*
. . . with breakfast	. . . mit Frühstück *mit frewstewk*
. . . with full/half board	. . . mit Vollpension/ Halbpension *mit follpenziohn/halp-* *pensiohn*
. . . for children	. . . für Kinder *fewr kinder*
Does that include breakfast/ VAT?	Ist das mit Frühstück/ Mehrwertsteuer? *ist das mit frewstewk/* *mairvairt-shtoyer?*
That's too expensive	Das ist mir zu teuer *das ist meer tsoo toyer*
I'd like a single room . . .	Ich möchte ein Einzelzimmer . . . *ikh murkhter I-n I-ntsel-* *tsimmer . . .*
We'd like a double room . . .	Wir möchten ein Doppelzimmer . . . *veer murkhten yn doppel-* *tsimmer . . .*
. . . with a bath	. . . mit Bad *mit baat*
. . . with a shower	. . . mit Dusche *mit doosher*
. . . with a balcony	. . . mit Balkon *mit balkohn*
Do you have any vacancies?	Haben Sie Zimmer frei? *haaben zee tsimer fry?*

Accommodation

I/we have a reservation	Ich habe/wir haben ein Zimmer reserviert *ikh haaber/veer haaben I-n tsimmer rezerveert*
My name is ...	Ich heiße ... *ikh hyser ...*

● You will often be asked to fill in a registration form (*Anmeldeformular*).

You may see:

Name	Name
Vorname	Forename
Nummer	Number
Straße	Road
Wohnort	Town
Postleitzahl (Plz)	postcode/zip code
Geburtsdatum	Date of birth
Geburtsort	Place of birth
Paßnummer	Passport number
Datum	Date
Unterschrift	Signature

May I see the room?	Darf ich das Zimmer sehen? *daarf ikh das tsimmer sai-en?*
It's too small/noisy	Es ist zu klein/laut *es ist tsoo klyn/lowt*
Can we have a child's cot?	Können wir ein Kinderbett haben? *kurnen veer I-n kinderbet haaben?*

Could you have my luggage brought to my room?	Könnten Sie bitte mein Gepäck auf mein Zimmer bringen lassen? *kurnten zee bitte myn gerpeck owf myn tsimmer bringen lassen?*
Where can I park my car?	Wo kann ich mein Auto parken? *voh kan ikh myn owtoh parken?*
We'll take it	Wir nehmen es *veer naimen es*

You may hear:

Wir haben kein Zimmer mehr frei *veer haaben kyn tsimmer mair fry*	We have no more rooms free
Wir haben keine Doppelzimmer mehr frei *veer haaben kyner dopeltsimmer mair fry*	We have no double rooms free
Wie heißen Sie? *vee hyssen zee?*	What is your name?
Bitte füllen Sie das Anmeldeformular aus *bitter fewlen zee das anmelderformoolaar ows*	Please fill in the registration form
Darf ich Ihren Paß sehen? *daarf ikh eeren pass sai-en?*	May I see your passport?
Unterschreiben Sie, bitte *oontershryben zee, bitter*	Please sign this
Wie lange bleiben Sie? *vee langer blyben zee?*	How long are you staying?
Ihre Zimmernummer ist . . . *eerer tsimmer-noomer ist . . .*	Your room number is . . .

Room service and meals

What time is breakfast/evening meal?	Wann gibt es Frühstück/Abendessen? *van gipt ess frewstewk/aabendessen?*
Can we have breakfast in our room?	Können wir auf unserem Zimmer frühstücken? *kurnen veer owf oonzerem tsimmer frewstewkern?*
Please wake me at ... o'clock	Bitte wecken Sie mich um ... Uhr *bitter veken zee mikh um ... oor*
May I have ...?	Kann ich ... haben? *kan ikh ... haaben?*
... a bath towel	... ein Badetuch *I-n baadertookh*
... some clothes hangers	... einige Kleiderbügel *I-niger klyderbewgel*
... another pillow	... noch ein Kopfkissen *nokh I-n kopf-kissen*
... some soap	... Seife *zyfer*
... an ashtray	... einen Aschenbecher *I-nen ashen-bekher*
... an extra blanket	... eine extra Decke *I-ner extra dekker*
... a needle and thread	... eine Nadel und etwas Faden *I-ner naadel oont etvas faaden*
Can you get me a taxi?	Können Sie mir ein Taxi bestellen? *kurnen zee meer I-n taxi beshtelen?*

Can I phone direct from my room?	Kann ich von meinem Zimmer durchwählen? *kan ikh von mynem tsimmer doorkh-vailen?*
Is there any post for me?	Ist Post für mich da? *ist posst fewr mikh daa?*
My room number is . . .	Meine Zimmernummer ist . . . *myner tsimmer-noomer ist . . .*
What is my room number?	Welche Zimmernummer habe ich? *velkher tsimmer-noomer haaber ikh?*
Could I have my key please?	Den Schlüssel, bitte *dain shlewssel bitter*
Can I leave this in the safe?	Kann ich das im Safe deponieren? *kan ikh das im 'safe' deponeeren?*
Where is the socket for the shaver?	Wo ist die Steckdose für den Rasierapparat? *voh ist dee shtek-dohzer fewr dain razeer-aparaat?*
I want these clothes cleaned	Ich möchte diese Kleider reinigen lassen *ikh murkhter deezer klyder rynigen lassen*
I need them today/tonight/ tomorrow	Ich brauche sie heute/heute abend/morgen *ikh browkher zee hoyter/ hoyter aabent/morgen*
Are there any messages for me?	Hat jemand eine Nachricht für mich hinterlassen? *hat yaimant I-ner nakh-rikht fewr mikh hinterlassen?*
Is there room-service?	Gibt es Zimmerservice? *gipt es tsimmer-sairvis?*

Queries and complaints

The . . . is broken/doesn't work/is blocked	. . . funktioniert nicht/ist kaputt/ist verstopft *foonktsioneert nikht/ist kapoot/ist fairshtopft*
. . . heating	Die Heizung . . . *dee hytsoong . . .*
. . . light	Das Licht . . . *das likht . . .*
. . . plug (electric)	Der Stecker . . . *dair shteker . . .*
. . . shutter	Der Fensterladen . . . *dair fensterlaaden . . .*
. . . shower	Die Dusche . . . *dee doosher . . .*
. . . socket	Die Steckdose . . . *dee shtekdohzer . . .*
. . . television	Der Fernseher . . . *dair fairnzai-er . . .*
. . . wash-basin	Das Waschbecken . . . *das vashbeken . . .*
. . . bath	Die Badewanne . . . *dee baadervanner . . .*
. . . toilet	Die Toilette . . . *dee twaletter . . .*
. . . air conditioning	die Klimaanlage . . . *dee kleema-anlaager . . .*
. . . radio	das Radio . . . *das raadio . . .*
How does . . . work?	Wie funktioniert . . . ? *vee foonktsioneert . . . ?*
The window is jammed	Das Fenster klemmt *das fenster klemmt*

The tap (faucet) is dripping	Der Wasserhahn tropft *dair vasserhaan tropft*
The bulb has blown	Die Birne ist kaputt *dee beerner ist kapoot*
My room has not been cleaned	Mein Zimmer wurde nicht geputzt *myn tsimmer voorder nikht gerpootst*
Can you get it repaired?	Können Sie es reparieren lassen? *kurnen zee es repareeren lassen?*
There isn't any hot water	Es gibt kein warmes Wasser *es gipt kyn vaarmes vasser*
Where is the . . . ?	Wo ist . . . ? *voh ist . . . ?*
. . . dining-room	. . . der Speisesaal . . . ? *dair shpyzer-zaal . . . ?*
. . . lift	. . . der Fahrstuhl *dair faar-shtool*
. . . toilet	. . . die Toilette *dee twaletter*
Do you have any . . . ?	Haben Sie . . . ? *haaben zee . . . ?*
. . . writing paper	. . . Schreibpapier *shryp-papeer*
. . . envelopes	. . . Briefumschläge *breef-oomshlaiger*
. . . stamps	. . . Briefmarken *breefmaarken*
Can I make a phone call from here?	Kann ich von hier telefonieren? *kan ikh fon heer telefohneeren?*

Checking out

May I have the bill?	Können Sie mir bitte die Rechnung geben? *kurnen zee meer bitter dee rekhnoong gaiben?*
Can I pay by credit card?	Kann ich mit Kreditkarte bezahlen? *kan ikh mit kredeetkarter bertsaalen?*
I'm/we're leaving . . .	Ich fahre/wir fahren . . . ab *ikh faarer/veer faaren . . . ap*
. . . tomorrow	. . . morgen . . . *morgen*
. . . today	. . . heute . . . *hoyter*
Can we have our luggage brought down?	Können Sie unser Gepäck herunterbringen lassen? *kurnen zee oonzer gerpek hairoonter-bringen lassen?*
I must leave at once	Ich muß sofort abreisen *ikh moos zofort apryzen*
Is everything included?	Ist alles inbegriffen? *ist all-es inbergriffen?*
I think you've made a mistake (in the bill)	Ich glaube, Sie haben sich verrechnet *ikh glowber zee haaben sikh fair-rekhnet*
Can you call a taxi?	Können Sie ein Taxi bestellen? *kurnen zee I-n taxi bershtellen?*
Here's the forwarding address	Hier is meine Nachsendeadresse *heer ist myner nakh-zender-adresser*
I'm in a hurry	Ich habe es eilig *ikh haaber es I-lig*

Youth hostel

- You can use your British Youth Hostel Association card in Germany, Austria and Switzerland if you attach a recent passport photo to it.
- There are separate dormitories for men and women, and you are advised to take your own sleeping bag.

Where is the youth hostel?	Wo ist die Jugendherberge, bitte? *voh ist dee yoogent-hairbairger, bitter?*
Do you have any beds free?	Haben Sie noch Plätze frei? *haaben zee nokh pletser fry?*
We'd like to stay 1/2 nights	Wir möchten eine Nacht/zwei Nächte bleiben *veer murkhten I-ner nakht/tsvy nekhter blyben*

There's ...	Wir sind ... *veer zint ...*
... 1/2 boys	... ein Junge/zwei Jungen *I-n yoonger/tsvy yoongen*
... 1/2 girls	... ein/zwei Mädchen *I-n/tsvy maidkhen*
... 1/2 adults	... ein/zwei Erwachsene *I-n/tsvy airvakhsener*
... 1/2 children	... ein Kind/zwei Kinder *I-n kint/tsvy kinder*

Here's my membership card	Hier ist mein Ausweis *heer ist myn owsvys*
We need bed linen	Wir brauchen Bettwäsche *veer browkhen betvesher*
We'd like supper and breakfast	Wir möchten Abendbrot und Frühstück *veer murkhten aabentbroht oont frewstewk*

Accommodation

Where is . . . ?	Wo ist . . . ? *voh ist . . . ?*
. . . our dormitory	. . . unser Schlafraum *oonzer shlaafrowm*
. . . the kitchen	. . . die Küche *dee kewkher*
. . . the shower	. . . die Dusche *dee doosher*
. . . the toilet	. . . die Toilette *dee twaletter*
. . . the washroom	. . . der Waschraum *dair vashrowm*

You may hear:

Wir sind voll belegt *veer zint fol berlaigt*	We're full up
Wieviele Personen? *veefeeler pairzohnen?*	How many people?
Wieviele Nächte? *veefeeler nekhter?*	How many nights?
Wie lange wollen Sie bleiben? *vee langer vollen zee blyben?*	How long do you want to stay?
Ihre Ausweise, bitte *eerer owsvyzer bitter*	May I have your cards, please?
Wollen Sie Bettwäsche leihen? *vollen zee betvesher lyen?*	Do you want bed linen?
Brauchen Sie Schlafsäcke? *browkhen zee schlaafzeker?*	Do you need sleeping-bags?
Welche Mahlzeiten wollen Sie? *velkher maaltsyten vollen zee?*	Which meals do you want?

Camping

- There are thousands of campsites in Germany, Austria and Switzerland: some, in mountain areas, are open all year round. The tourist office can help you to find a suitable site. It is illegal to camp without permission.

We're looking for a campsite	Wir suchen einen Campingplatz *veer zookhen I-nen kempingplats*
Can we camp here?	Können wir hier zelten? *kurnen veer heer tselten?*
Are there any other campsites nearby?	Gibt es andere Campingplätze in der Nähe? *gipt es anderer kempingpletser in dair nai-er?*
Do you have any vacancies for . . . ?	Haben Sie Platz für . . . ? *haaben zee plats fewr . . . ?*
. . . a tent	. . . ein Zelt *I-n tselt*
. . . a caravan	. . . einen Wohnwagen *I-nen vohnvaagen*
. . . a motor-home	. . . ein Wohnmobil *I-n vohn mobeel*
How much does it cost for . . . ?	Wieviel kostet es für . . . ? *veefeel kostet es fewr . . . ?*
. . . a night	. . . eine Nacht *I-ner nakht*
. . . a week	. . . eine Woche *I-ner vokher*
. . . one person	. . . eine Person *I-ner pairsohn*
. . . a car	. . . ein Auto *I-n owtoh*

Does that include everything?	Ist alles im Preis inbegriffen? *ist ales im prys inbergriffen?*
Is/are there . . . ?	Gibt es . . . ? *gipt es . . . ?*
. . . cooking facilities	. . . Kochgelegenheiten *kokh-gerlaigenhyten*
. . . electricity	. . . Stromanschluß *shtrohm-anshloos*
. . . a shop	. . . einen Laden *I-nen laaden*
. . . showers	. . . Duschen *dooshen*
. . . a swimming pool	. . . ein Schwimmbad *I-n shvimbaad*
. . . washing machines	. . . Waschmaschinen *vashmasheenen*
Where can I get butane gas?	Wo kann ich Butangas berkommen? *voh kan ikh bootaangas berkomen*
Are there discounts for children?	Gibt es Rabatt für die Kinder? *gipt es rabaat fewr dee kinnder?*
Do you have . . . ?	Haben Sie . . . ? *haaben zee . . . ?*
. . . ice	. . . Eis *I-s*
. . . gas	. . . Butangas *bootaangas*
Does the campsite close at night?	Schließt der Campingplatz nachts? *shleest dair kemping-plats nakhts?*

Apartments

- Cleaning is always included in the price.

I'd like an apartment ...	Ich möchte eine Ferienwohnung ... *ikh murkhter yner fairien-vohnoong ...*
... with one bedroom	... mit einem Schlafzimmer *mit I-nem shlaaf-tsimmer*
... with two bedrooms	... mit zwei Schlafzimmern *mit tsvy shlaaf-tsimmern*
... for three people	... für drei Personen *fewr dry pairzohnen*
... for six people	... für sechs Personen *fewr zekhs pairzohnen*
... for a week	... für eine Woche *few I-ner vokher*
... for a fortnight	... für zwei Wochen *fewr tsvy vokhen*
Which floor is it on?	In welchem Stock ist es? *in velkhem shtok ist es?*
Is ... included?	Ist ... inbegriffen? *ist ... inbegriffen?*
... everything	... alles ... *all-es*
... the gas	... das Gas ... *das gas*
... the water	... das Wasser ... *das vasser*
... the electricity	... der Strom ... *dair shtrohm*

When ... ?	Wann ... ? *van ... ?*
... is it cleaned	... wird geputzt *veert gerpootst*
... is the rubbish collected	... kommt die Müllabfuhr *kommt dee mewl-apfoor*

Does it have ... ?	Gibt es ... ? *gipt es ... ?*
... heating	... Heizung *hytsoong*
... a fridge	... einen Kühlschrank *I-nen kewlshrank*
... bedclothes	... Bettzeug *bet-tsoyg*
... crockery	... Geschirr *gersheer*
... cutlery	... Besteck *bershtek*
... a washing machine	... eine Waschmaschine *I-ner vashmasheener*

Is it fully equipped?	Ist es voll ausgestattet? *ist es fol owsgershtattet?*
Is it electric or gas?	Ist es elektrisch oder gas? *ist es elektrish ohder gas?*
I need ...	Ich brauche ... *ikh browkher ...*
... an electrician	... einen Elektriker *I-nen elektriker*
... a plumber	... einen Klempner *I-nen klempner*
... a gas man	... einen Gasmann *I-nen gasman*

- There is a special **What's on the menu?** section listing items of food and German specialities on page 155.
- It is possible to buy a meal at any time of day, and well into the evening, in Germany, Austria and Switzerland. You will find foreign restaurants (particularly Italian) and fast-food cafeterias as well as the usual cafés and pubs where you can eat *gut bürgerlich* (good home cooking).
- Each area has its own specialities of dishes, breads, cakes, sausages, and beers or wines.
- In all but fast-food shops and snack-bars, there will be waiters or waitresses.
- German law allows children and young people to buy alcohol (but not spirits) at 14 if accompanied by an adult, 16 if not. Children are allowed in pubs.

Places to eat and drink

Bierhalle/Bierstube   Rather like a pub or tavern. The emphasis is on beer rather than food.

Café/Café-Konditorei   Coffee shop. The cheapest are self-service cafés where the customers stand at small high tables. Normal cafés are often linked to a *Konditorei*, a cake/pastry shop. If you want a slice of cake with your drink, make your selection out in the shop (unless you know the name of what you want); you will be given a piece of paper (*ein Zettel*) which you give to the waitress when you place your drinks order.

Gasthaus/Gasthof   Inn. Found in the country or in small towns, with snacks, full meals and drinks on offer. Don't sit at a table marked *Stammtisch* – it's reserved for a particular group of regular customers.

Gaststätte   Restaurant

Kaffeehaus   Café, in Austria.

Raststätte/Rasthof   Motorway services and restaurant.

Ratskeller/Ratstube   Café or restaurant near to, or in the cellar of the town hall.

Schnellimbiß/Imbiß   Snack bar, selling mainly beer and sausages.

Weinstube   Rather like a Gasthof; found in wine-producing areas.

You may see:	
Heute Ruhetag	Closed today
Montag Betriebsruhe	Closed on Mondays
Durchgehend warme Küche	Hot meals available all day
Straßenverkauf	Take-away
Zum Mitnehmen	Take-away
Reserviert	Reserved
Stammtisch	Table reserved for landlord and regulars (in pubs)

Meals

Breakfast (*das Frühstück*): a fairly substantial meal of bread, rolls, cheese, cold meats and sausages, and jam, accompanied by coffee, tea, milk, and/or fruit juice.

Lunch (*das Mittagessen*): this is often the main meal of the day, and is usually accompanied by salads. It is often not followed by a pudding.

Evening meal (*das Abendessen*): when taken at home, it is often rather like breakfast; when guests are invited, or in restaurants, a cooked meal is more normal.

Afternoon tea (*Kaffee und Kuchen*): this is often taken at weekends, and usually consists of coffee and various cakes/pastries.

Reservations

Have you got a table free?	Haben Sie einen Tisch frei? *haaben zee I-nen tish fry?*
I'd like to reserve a table for 4	Ich möchte einen Tisch für vier reservieren *ikh murkhter I-nen tish fewr feer rezerveeren*
We're coming at 9	Wir kommen um neun *veer kommen oom noyn*

We'd like a table . . .	Wir möchten einen Tisch . . . *veer murkhten I-nen tish . . .*
. . . by the window	. . . neben dem Fenster *naiben daim fenster*
. . . in a no-smoking area	. . . in der Nichtraucherecke *in dair nikht-rowkher-eker*
. . . outside	. . . im Freien *im fryen*
. . . on the terrace	. . . auf der Terrasse *owf dair tairasser*

35

My name is . . .	Ich heiße . . . *ikh hysser . . .*
Can I pay by credit card?	Kann ich mit Kreditkarte bezahlen? *kan ikh mit kredeetkarter bertsaalen?*
I have a reservation	Ich habe reserviert *ikh haaber resairveert*

Ordering

● When ordering a meal in an inn it is worth bearing in mind the main courses are substantial; a starter and a pudding are often unnecessary, unless you're very hungry.

Waiter/Waitress!	Herr Ober/Bedienung! *hair ohber/berdeenoong!*
May I have the menu, please?	Kann ich die Speisekarte haben, bitte? *kan ikh dee shpyzer-kaarter haaben, bitter?*
May we have the wine list, please?	Können wir die Getränkekarte haben, bitte? *Kurnen veer dee gertrenkerkaarter haaben, bitter?*
I'm/we're ready to order now	Ich möchte/wir möchten jetzt bestellen *ikh murkhter/veer murkhten yetst bershtellen*
I/we haven't decided yet	Ich bin/wir sind noch nicht fertig *ikh bin/veer zint nokh nikht fairtig*
Do you have any . . . ?	Haben Sie . . . ? *haaben zee . . . ?*
I/we'll order something to drink first	Ich bestelle/wir bestellen zuerst etwas zu trinken *ikh bershtelle/veer bershtellen tsoo-airst etvas tsoo trinken*

I'd just like a snack	Ich möchte nur eine Kleinigkeit essen
	ikh murkhte noor I-ner klynigkyt essen
What do you recommend?	Was empfehlen Sie?
	vas empfailen zee?
Do you have any local dishes?	Haben Sie Gerichte aus der Gegend?
	haaben zee gerikhter ows dair gaigent?
What is that?	Was ist das für ein Gericht?
	vas ist das fewr yn gerikht?
Is salad/vegetables included?	Ist das mit Salat/Gemüse?
	ist das mit zalaat/germewser?
Do you have a children's menu?	Haben Sie einen Kinderteller?
	haaben zee I-nen kinnderteller?
Do you have any vegetarian dishes?	Haben Sie vegetarische Gerichte?
	haaben zee vegetaarisher gerikhter?

I'm not allowed to eat ...	Ich darf ... nicht essen.
	ikh daarf ... nikht essen
... eggs	... Eier ...
	I-er
... fat	... Fett ...
	fet
... flour	... Mehl ...
	mail
... sugar	... Zucker ...
	tsooker
We'd all/both like ...	Wir möchten alle/beide ...
	veer murkhten aler/byder ...

I'd like the menu at 30DM/ the dish of the day	Ich hätte gern das Menü zu dreißig Mark/das Tagesgericht *ikh hetter gairn das menew tsoo drysig mark/das taages-gerikht*
That's for her/him/me	Das ist für sie/ihn/mich *das ist fewr zee/een/mikh*
The same for me, please	Das gleiche für mich, bitte *das glykher fewr mikh, bitter*
Could I have . . . instead?	Kann ich statt dessen . . . haben? *kan ikh shtat dessen . . . haaben?*

May I have . . . ?	Kann ich . . . haben? *kan ikh . . . haaben?*
. . . some more	. . . etwas mehr . . . *etvas mair*
. . . some (more) bread	. . . (noch) etwas Brot . . . *(nokh) etvas broht*
. . . some (more) butter	. . . (noch) etwas Butter . . . *(nokh) etvas booter*
. . . a (-nother) beer	. . . (noch) ein Bier . . . *(nokh) I-n beer*
. . . a (-nother) pot of coffee	. . . (noch) ein Kännchen Kaffee . . . *(nokh) I-n kenshen kafai*
. . . a (-nother) cup of tea	. . . (noch) eine Tasse Tee . . . *(nokh) I-ner tasser tai*
. . . a (-nother) glass of wine	. . . (noch) ein Glas Wein . . . *(nokh) I-n glaas vyn*
. . . a (-nother) portion of . . .	. . . (noch) eine Portion . . . *(nokh) I-ner portsiohn . . .*

No more, thank you	Nichts mehr, danke *nikhts mair, danker*

Problems and Queries

I ordered . . .	Ich habe . . . bestellt *ikh haaber . . . bershtelt*
We've been waiting for 20 minutes	Wir warten schon seit zwanzig Minuten *veer vaarten shohn zyt tsvantsig minooten*

May I have a (-nother) . . .	Kann ich . . . haben? *kan ikh . . . haaben?*

. . . fork	. . . eine (andere) Gabel . . . *I-ner (anderer) gaabel*
. . . glass	. . . ein (anderes) Glas . . . *I-n (anderes) glaas*
. . . knife	. . . ein (anderes) Messer . . . *I-n (anderes) messer*
. . . spoon	. . . einen (anderen) Löffel . . . *I-nen (anderen) lurfel*

This isn't clean	Das ist nicht sauber *das ist nikht zowber*

This is . . .	Das ist . . . *das ist . . .*

. . . burnt	. . . angebrannt *angerbrant*
. . . cold	. . . kalt *kalt*
. . . not fresh	. . . nicht frisch *nikht frish*
. . . overcooked	. . . verkocht *fairkokht*
. . . too salty/sweet	. . . zu salzig/süß *tsoo zaltsig/sews*
. . . underdone	. . . nicht gar *nikht gaar*

Paying the bill

- In restaurants, the service charge is usually included in the bill, although you may of course leave a little extra by rounding up the amount if you were especially pleased by the service you received.

May I have the bill, please?	Ich möchte zahlen, bitte *ikh murkhter tsaalen, bitter*
We're paying together/separately	Wir bezahlen zusammen/getrennt *veer bertsaalen tsoozammen/gertrent*
There seems to be a mistake in the bill	Ich glaube, Sie haben sich verrechnet *ikh glowber, zee haaben zikh fairekhnet*
What is this amount for?	Wofür steht dieser Betrag? *vohfewr stait deezer bertraag?*
Does that include service?	Ist das mit Bedienung? *ist das mit berdeenoong?*
Keep the change	Stimmt so *shtimmt zoh*
Do you accept traveller's cheques/credit cards?	Nehmen Sie Reiseschecks/Kreditkarten? *naimen zee ryzer-sheks/kredeet-kaarten?*
I don't have enough cash	Ich habe nicht genug in bar *ikh haaber nikht gernoog in baar*
You've given me the wrong change	Sie haben mir falsch herausgegeben *zee haaben meer falsh hairowsgergaiben*
May I have a receipt?	Kann ich eine Quittung haben? *kan ikh I-ner kvittoong haaben?*

Eating out

You may hear:

Bitte schön?
bitter shurn?

Was darf es sein?   What would you like?
vas darf es zyn?

Was möchten Sie?
vas murkhten zee?

Haben Sie schon gewählt?
haaben zee shohn gervelt?

Haben Sie etwas   Have you decided yet?
ausgesucht?
haaben zee etvas
awsgezookht?

Sonst noch etwas?   Anything else?
zonst nokh etvas?

... haben wir nicht mehr   We haven't any more ...
... haaben veer nikht mair

Möchten Sie einen   Would you like a dessert?
Nachtisch?
murkhten zee I-nen
nakhtish?

You may see:

Hauptgerichte	main courses
hausgemacht	home-made
Imbisse	snacks
im Preis inbegriffen	included in the price
inklusive Bedienung und Mehrwertsteuer	service and VAT (sales tax) included
mit Beilage	with salad or vegetables
Nachspeisen	desserts
nur auf Bestellung	to order only
Spezialität des Hauses	speciality of the house
Tagesgedeck/Tagesmenü	set menu of the day
Tagesgericht	dish of the day

41

Drinks

Non-Alcoholic

I'd like a/an . . .	Ich möchte . . . *ikh murkhter . . .*
. . . apple juice	. . . einen Apfelsaft *I-nen apfelzaft*
. . . blackcurrant juice	. . . einen Johannisbeersaft *I-nen yohanisbairzaft*
. . . chocolate	. . . eine Schokolade *I-ner shokolaader*
. . . coffee	. . . einen Kaffee *I-nen kafai*
. . . Coke	. . . ein Cola *I-n kohla*
. . . fruit juice	. . . einen Fruchtsaft *I-nen frookhtzaft*
. . . lemonade	. . . eine Limonade *I-ner limonaader*
. . . fizzy/still mineral water	. . . ein Mineralwasser mit/ ohne Kohlensäure *I-n mineraalvasser mit/ ohner kohlenzoyrer*
. . . orange juice	. . . einen Orangensaft *I-nen oranjenzaft*
. . . tea	. . . einen Tee *I-nen tai*
. . . herb tea	. . . einen Kräutertee *I-nen kroytertai*
. . . tomato juice	. . . einen Tomatensaft *I-nen tomaatenzaft*
. . . tonic water	. . . ein Tonic *I-n tonik*
a cup	eine Tasse *I-ner tasser*

a pot (holds about 2 cups)	ein Kännchen *I-n kenkhen*
a black coffee	einen schwarzen Kaffee *I-nen shvaartsen kafai*
with cream	mit Sahne *mit zaaner*
with milk	mit Milch *mit milkh*
decaffeinated	koffeinfrei *koffe-eenfry*
espresso	einen Espresso *I-nen espressoh*
with lemon	mit Zitrone *mit tsitrohner*

- Tea is served without milk unless requested.

Beer

- Almost every town in Germany has its brewery, and there are dozens of types of beer, some brewed only at particular times of the year.

I'd like ...	Ich möchte ... *ikh murkhter ...*
... a glass of ...	... ein Glas ... *I-n glaas*
... two glasses of ...	... zwei Gläser ... *tsvy glaizer*
... a bottle of ...	... eine Flasche ... *I-ner flasher*
... two bottles of ...	... zwei Flaschen ... *tsvy flaschen*
... a tankard (litre) ...	... eine Maß ... *I-ner maas*
... another beer, please ...	... noch ein Bier, bitte *nokh I-n beer bitter*

Altbier *altbeer*	a top-fermented, dark beer
Bier *beer*	beer
Bockbier *bokbeer*	} types of strong beer
Doppelbock *doppelbok*	
ein Dunkles *I-n doonkles*	a dark beer
ein Helles *I-n helles*	a light-coloured beer
Malzbier *maltsbeer*	dark, sweet, low in alcohol
Märzen *mairtsen*	a strong, light beer
Pils/Pilsener *pils/pilsner*	like lager – the commonest type of beer
... vom Faß *fom fass*	draught
Weißbier/Weizenbier *vysbeer/vytsenbeer*	a light, fizzy beer made from wheat

- In pubs, the waiter or waitress will often mark your beermat each time you order a drink – you pay at the end of the evening. Almost all pubs have a waiter service, and, unlike Britain, it is normal to drink sitting down. No-one stands at the bar.

Wine

- Germany, Austria and Switzerland all produce wine. If you are in a wine-producing region, all pubs and restaurants will stock locally-produced wines, although you may be able to buy wines from other parts of Europe too.
- The flabby, over-sweetened *Liebfraumilch* and *Hock* which are often the only German wines obtainable in most British supermarkets and off-licences, are unknown in Germany.

44

I'd like ...	Ich möchte ... *ikh murkhter ...*
... a glass of ...	... ein Glas ... *I-n glaas ...*
... a bottle of ...	... eine Flasche ... *I-ner flasher ...*
... red wine	... Rotwein *rohtvyn*
... white wine	... Weißwein *vysvyn*
... rosé	... Rosé *rohzay*
... sparkling wine/ champagne	... Sekt *zekt*
... white wine with soda/ mineral water	... ein Schorle *I-n shorler*

● You could also try *Schillerwein*, which is made by
fermenting white and red grapes together, or *Weißherbst*,
which is a very light wine made from bluish-skinned grapes.

Quality and Flavour

crisp	frisch/herb *frish/hairp*
dry	trocken *trocken*
fruity	fruchtig *frookhtig*
sweet	süß *zewss*
light	leicht *lykht*
full-bodied	vollmundig *follmoondig*
table-wine/'plonk'	Tafelwein *taafelvyn*

45

● *'Aus den Ländern der EG'* may be added. This indicates that most of the contents of the bottle are from other European countries; these wines are usually of very poor quality.

QbA *koo bai aa*	(Qualitätswein aus den bestimmten Anbaugebieten)	a blended wine from a certified region eg Mosel, Rhein
QmP *koo em pai*	(Qualitätswein mit Prädikat)	a quality wine with a title:
	Kabinett *kabinet*	high quality
	Spätlese *shpaitlaizer*	late vintage
	Auslese *owslaizer*	late vintage from specially selected bunches of grapes
	Beerenauslese *bairen-owslaizer*	made from selected over-ripe grapes
	Trockenbeerenauslese *trokenbairen-owslaizer*	made from grapes so over-ripe they are like raisins
	Eiswein *I-svyn*	an intense wine made from frozen grapes

● The QmP titles indicate stages, not of increasing quality, but of increasing intensity and, usually, sweetness. With most savoury foods, a *Kabinett* or dry (*trocken*) *Spätlese* is recommended.
● A *Qualitätswein* (quality wine) will also have the name of the village and the vineyard where it was produced:
eg *Eltviller Langenstück – Eltville* is the village, *Langenstück* is the vineyard.

Main Grape Varieties

White wines

Riesling *reezling*	fresh; older wines elegant
Silvaner *zilvaaner*	gentle flavour
Müller-Thurgau *mewler-toorgow*	fruity, rounded
Gewürztraminer *gervewrts-trameener*	tending to spicy flavour

Red wines

Spätburgunder *shpaitboorgoonder*	the *pinot noir*; can be quite full-bodied in a good year
Lemberger *lembairger*	can be dry, full-bodied, but varies according to vineyard (SW Germany only)
Portugieser *portoogeezer*	rounded flavour
Trollinger *trolinger*	fresh and fruity (SW Germany only)

Other Alcoholic Drinks

I'd like a/an/some . . .	Ich möchte . . . *ikh murkhter . . .*
. . . brandy	. . . einen Weinbrand *I-nen vynbrant*
. . . cider	. . . Apfelwein/Apfelmost *apfelvyn/apfelmosst*
. . . cognac	. . . einen Kognak *I-nen konyak*
. . . gin	. . . einen Gin *I-nen jin*

(**Doornkaat** (*doornkaat*) and **Steinhäger** (*shtynhaiger*) are the two best-known varieties)

. . . liqueur	. . . einen Likör *I-nen likur*
. . . port	. . . einen Portwein *I-nen portvyn*
. . . rum	. . . einen Rum *I-nen room*
. . . sherry	. . . einen Sherry *I-nen sherri*
. . . vermouth	. . . einen Wermut *I-nen vairmut*
. . . vodka	. . . einen Wodka *I-nen vodka*
. . . whisky	. . . einen Whisky *I-nen wiskee*
neat (straight)	pur *poor*
with ice (on the rocks)	mit Eis *mit I-s*

- German specialities include *Geist* (a clear spirit made from fruit eg *Kirschgeist* is the cherry variety), *Korn* (corn brandy) and *Schnaps* (a strong, clear brandy).

ENTERTAINMENT AND SPORT

- There is plenty to choose from in the way of entertainment in most German towns. Discos and other 'continuous' entertainments are usually open until late.
- Many more towns than in Britain or the USA have a theatre, and concert hall and opera or ballet companies. Booking is usually advisable.
- You can find out what's on from the tourist office, or from the local newspaper.
- Films are usually dubbed into German rather than subtitled.
- The German-speaking countries are well-known for their winter sports facilities. Germany has resorts not only in the Alps, but also in the Black Forest (*Schwarzwald*), and the Harz mountains. Both downhill (*Abfahrtslauf*) and cross-country skiing (*Langlauf*) are popular.

General enquiries and booking

What is there to do this evening?	Was ist heute abend los? *vas ist hoyter aabernt lohs?*
I'm interested in . . .	Ich interessiere mich für . . . *ikh interesseerer mikh fewr . . .*
. . . classical music	. . . klassische Musik *klassisher moozeek*
. . . pop music	. . . Popmusik *popmoozeek*
. . . jazz	. . . Jazz *jaz*
. . . folk music	. . . Volksmusik *folks-moozeek*
. . . films	. . . Filme *filmer*
I'd like to go. . .	Ich möchte . . . gehen *ikh murkhter . . . gai-en*
. . . to the cinema	. . . ins Kino . . . *ins keeno*
. . . to a disco	. . . in eine Disko . . . *in I-ner diskoh*
. . . to a nightclub	. . . in ein Nachtlokal . . . *in I-n nakht-lohkaal*
. . . to the theatre	. . . ins Theater . . . *ins tai-aater*
. . . to a concert	. . . in ein Konzert . . . *in I-n kontsert*
. . . to the opera	. . . in die Oper . . . *in dee ohper*
. . . the ballet	. . . ins Ballett . . . *ins balet*

Entertainment and sport

Can you recommend a disco/ a nightclub?	Können Sie eine Disko/ein Nachtlokal empfehlen?
	kurnen zee I-ner diskoh/yn nakht-lohkaal emp-failen?
Are there any tickets for this evening/tomorrow?	Gibt es Karten für heute abend/morgen?
	gipt es kaarten fewr hoyter aabent/ morgen?
How much are the tickets?	Was kosten die Karten?
	vas kosten dee kaarten?
When does it begin?	Wann beginnt es?
	van bergint es?
When does it end?	Wann ist es zu Ende?
	van ist es tsoo ender

I'd like 1/2 tickets . . .	Ich möchte eine Karte/2 Karten . . .
	ikh murkhter I-ner kaarter/ tsvy kaarten . . .

. . . for this evening	. . . für heute abend
	fewr hoyter aabent
. . . for tomorrow	. . . für morgen
	fewr morgen
. . . in the circle/stalls	. . . im Rang/Parkett
	im rang/parket

You may hear:

Ich empfehle . . .	I recommend . . .
ikh empfailer . . .	
Die Plätze sind ausverkauft	The tickets are sold out
dee pletser zint owsfairkowft	
Es gibt nur noch ein paar Plätze	There are just a few tickets left
es gipt noor nokh I-n paar pletser	

Concerts, opera, ballet

What's being played?	Was wird gespielt? *vas veert gershpeelt?*
Which opera/ballet is being performed?	Welche Oper/welches Ballett wird aufgeführt? *velkher ohper/velkhes balet veert owf-gerfewrt?*
Who's the soloist/conductor?	Wer ist der Solist/Dirigent? *vair ist dair zolist/dirigent?*
When is the interval?	Wann ist die Pause? *van ist dee powzer?*
How long does the interval last?	Wie lang dauert die Pause? *vee langer dowert dee powzer?*

Cinemas and Theatres

What's on at the cinema?	Was läuft im Kino? *vas loyft im keenoh?*
What's on at the theatre?	Was wird im Theater aufgeführt? *vas veert im tai-aarter owfgerfewrt?*
What sort of film/play is it?	Was für ein Film/Stück ist es? *vas fewr I-n film/shtewk ist es?*

You may see:	
Veranstaltungen	Events
Vorverkauf (-sstelle)	Advance booking (office)
Heute	Today
Ausverkauft	Sold out
Letzte Vorstellung	Last showing (of film)
Nächste Aufführung	Next performance (of play, etc.)

Is it . . . ?	Ist es . . . ? *ist es . . . ?*
. . . a comedy	. . . eine Komödie *I-ner kommurdi-er*
. . . a musical	. . . ein Musical *I-n moozikal*
. . . a horror film	. . . ein Horrorfilm *I-n horohrfilm*
. . . a thriller	. . . ein Krimi *I-n krimmi*
. . . a German film	. . . ein deutscher Film *I-n doycher film*
. . . subtitled	. . . mit Untertiteln *mit oonter-teetln*
. . . dubbed	. . . synchronisiert *zewn-khronizeert*
Who is in it?	Wer sind die Schauspieler? *vair zint dee show-shpeeler?*
Who wrote the play?	Wer hat das Stück geschrieben? *vair hat das shtewk gershreeben?*
Where is the cloakroom?	Wo ist die Garderobe? *voh ist dee gaarder-rohber?*
May I have a programme?	Kann ich bitte ein Programm haben? *kan ikh bitter I-n prohgram haaben?*

Discos and nightclubs

Is there a good disco?	Gibt es eine gute Disko? *gipt es I-ner gooter discoh?*
Would you like to dance?	Möchten Sie tanzen? *murkhten zee tantsen?*
Is there a floor show?	Gibt es ein Show? *gipt es I-n 'show'?*

53

Meeting people

- It's not difficult to make friends in Germany. It will be especially appreciated if you try to do so in German! Two sorts of phrases are provided here:
- The first, marked **P** (=*Polite*) uses the more formal word for 'you' (*Sie*); Adults talking to adults, or young people talking to adults they don't know, should use this list initially.
- The second, marked **F** (=*Friends*), uses the familiar *Du* for 'you', and is used by teenagers, and by friends of any age.

Good morning	Guten Morgen *gooten morgen*
Good afternoon	Guten Tag *gooten taag*
Good evening	Guten Abend *gooten aabent*
Goodbye (in person)	Auf Wiedersehen *owf veederzai-en*
(on phone)	Auf Wiederhören *owf veederhuren*
What's your name?	(P) Wie heißen Sie? *vee hysen zee?* (F) Wie heißt du? *vee hyst doo?*
My name is ...	Ich heiße ... *ikh hyser ...*
How are you?	(P) Wie geht es Ihnen? *vee gait es eenen?* (F) Wie geht's? *vee gaits?*
Fine, thanks. And you?	(P) Gut, danke. Und Ihnen? *goot, danker. oont eenen?* (F) Gut, danke. Und dir? *goot, danker. oont deer?*

Pleased to meet you	Freut mich *froyt mikh*
Where are you staying at the moment?	(P) Wo wohnen Sie zur Zeit? *voh vohnen zee tsoor tsyt?* (F) Wo wohnst du zur Zeit? *voh vohnst doo tsoor tsyt?*
I'm staying . . .	Ich wohne . . . *ikh vohner . . .*
Where do you come from?	(P) Woher kommen Sie? *voh-hair kommen zee?* (F) Woher kommst du? *voh-hair kommst doo?*
I'm from . . .	Ich komme aus . . . *ikh kommer ows . . .*
. . . America	. . . Amerika *amerika*
. . . Australia	. . . Australien *owstraalien*
. . . Britain	. . . Großbritannien *grohs-britaanien*
. . . Canada	. . . Kanada *kanada*
. . . Ireland	. . . Irland *eerlant*
Do you like it here?	(P) Gefällt es Ihnen hier? *gerfelt es eenen heer?* (F) Gefällt es dir hier? *gerfelt es deer heer?*
Are you here on holiday?	(P) Sind Sie auf Urlaub hier? *zint zee owf oorlowp heer?* (F) Bist du auf Urlaub hier? *bist doo owf oorlowp heer?*

I'm on a business trip	Ich bin auf Geschäftsreise *ikh bin owf gersheftsryzer*
I work for ...	Ich arbeite bei ... *ikh aarbyter by ...*
Are you on your own?	(P) Sind Sie allein? *zint zee alyn?* (F) Bist du allein? *bist doo alyn?*

My ... is here too	... ist auch hier *... ist owkh heer*
... boyfriend	Mein Freund ... *myn froynt*
... brother	Mein Bruder ... *myn brooder*
... family	Meine Familie ... *myner fameeli-er*
... father	Mein Vater ... *myn faater*
... girlfriend	Meine Freundin ... *myner froyndin*
... husband	Mein Mann ... *myn man*
... mother	Meine Mutter ... *myner mooter*
... parents	Meine Eltern ... *myner eltern*
... sister	Meine Schwester ... *myner shvester*
... wife	Meine Frau ... *myner frow*

Do you have a light please?	(P) Haben Sie Feuer, bitte? *haaben zee foyer bitter?* (F) Hast du Feuer, bitte? *hast doo foyer bitter?*

Would you like a cigarette?	(P) Möchten Sie eine Zigarette? *murkhten zee I-ner tsigaretter?*
	(F) Möchtest du eine Zigarette? *murkhtest doo I-ner tsigarretter?*
I'm afraid I don't/haven't	Leider nicht *lyder nikht*
Would you like a drink?	(P) Möchten Sie etwas trinken? *murkhten zee etvas trinken?*
	(F) Möchtest du etwas trinken? *murkhtest doo etvas trinken?*
Are you waiting for someone?	(P) Warten Sie auf jemanden? *vaarten zee owf yaimanden?*
	(F) Wartest du auf jemanden? *vaartest doo owf yaimanden?*
Are you free this evening?	(P) Haben Sie heute abend Zeit? *haaben zee hoyter aabent tsyt?*
	(F) Hast du heute abend Zeit? *hast doo hoyter aabent tsyt?*
I'm sorry, I'm not	Leider nicht *lyder nikht*
How about tomorrow?	Und morgen? *oont morgen?*

Would you like to go to a disco?	(P) Möchten Sie in eine Disko gehen? *murkhten zee in I-ner disko gai-en?*
	(F) Möchtest du in eine Disko gehen? *murkhtest doo in I-ner disko gai-en?*
Would you like to come with me/us?	(P) Kommen Sie mit? *kommen zee mit?*
	(F) Kommst du mit? *kommst doo mit?*
Would you like to go for a drink?	(P) Möchten Sie einen trinken gehen? *murkhten zee I-nen trinken gai-en?*
	(F) Möchtest du einen trinken gehen? *murkhtest doo I-nen trinken gai-en?*
Yes, I would	Ja, gerne *yaa, gairner*
I'd rather ...	Ich würde lieber ... *ikh vewrder leeber ...*
Where shall we meet?	Wo treffen wir uns? *voh treffen veer oons?*
At what time?	Um wieviel Uhr? *oom veefeel oor?*
I'll pick you up	(P) Ich hole Sie ab *ikh hohler zee ab*
	(F) Ich hole dich ab *ikh hohler dikh ab*
What is your address/phone number?	Wie ist Ihre (P)/deine (F) Adresse/Telefonnummer? *vee ist eerer/dyner adresser/ telefohn-noomer?*

Would you like to come over . . . ?	(P) Möchten Sie . . . zu uns kommen? *murkhten zee . . . tsoo oons kommen?* (F) Möchtest du . . . zu uns kommen? *murkhtest doo . . . tsoo oons kommen?*
. . . this evening	. . . heute abend *hoyter aabent*
. . . tomorrow	. . . morgen *morgen*
. . . on Saturday	. . . am Samstag *am zamztaag*
. . . for a glass of wine/beer	. . . auf ein Glas Wein/Bier *owf I-n glaas vyn/beer*
. . . for lunch	. . . zum Mittagessen *tsoom mitaagessen*
. . . for dinner	. . . zum Abendessen *tsoom aabentessen*
. . . to a party	. . . auf eine Party *owf I-ner partee*
At what time?	Um wieviel Uhr? *oom veefeel oor?*
At eight	Um acht *oom akht*
At about nine	Gegen neun *gaigen noyn*
I'm afraid we must leave now	Leider müssen wir jetzt gehen *lyder mewsen veer yetst gai-en*
It was lovely	Es war schön *es vaar shurn*
I've enjoyed it!	Es hat mir Spaß gemacht! *es hat meer shpaas germakht*

Sport

I'd like to see . . .	Ich möchte . . . sehen *ikh murkhter . . . sai-en*
. . . a football match	. . . ein Fußballspiel *I-n foosbal-shpeel*
. . . a tennis match	. . . ein Tennisspiel *I-n tennis-shpeel*
. . . some horse-racing	. . . Pferderennen *pfairder-rennen*
Who's playing?	Wer spielt? *vair shpeelt?*
When does it start?	Wann beginnt es? *van berginnt es?*
How much are the tickets?	Was kostet der Eintritt? *vas kostet dair I-ntrit?*
Can you get me a ticket?	Können Sie mir eine Karte besorgen? *kurnen zee meer I-ner kaarter bezorgen?*
Can you get us some tickets?	Können Sie uns Karten besorgen? *kurnen zee oons kaarten berzorgen?*
What are the opening times?	Wie sind die Öffnungszeiten? *vee sint dee urfnoongs- tsyten?*
Is it an open-air or an indoor pool?	Ist es ein Freibad oder ein Hallenbad? *ist es I-n frybaat ohder I-n hallenbaat?*
Is it heated?	Ist es geheizt? *ist es gerhytst?*
Can one swim in the lake/ river?	Kann man im See/Fluß schwimmen? *kan man im zai/floos shvimmen?*

Is there any fishing near here?	Kann man hier in der Nähe angeln? *kan man heer in dair nai-er angeln?*
Do I need a fishing permit?	Braucht man einen Angelschein? *browkht man I-nen angelshyn?*
How do I get a permit?	Wie bekomme ich einen Schein? *vee berkommer ikh I-nen shyn?*

I'd like to play . . .	Ich möchte . . . spielen *ikh murkhter . . . shpeelen*
Where can we play . . . ?	Wo können wir . . . spielen? *vo kurnen veer . . . shpeelen?*
Can I play . . . ?	Kann ich . . . spielen? *kan ikh . . . shpeelen?*

. . . golf	. . . Golf . . . *golf*
. . . tennis	. . . Tennis . . . *tennis*
. . . football	. . . Fußball . . . *foosbal*

What does it cost per . . . ?	Was kostet es pro . . . ? *vas kostet es pro . . . ?*

. . . day	. . . Tag *taag*
. . . game	. . . Spiel *shpeel*
. . . hour	. . . Stunde *shtoonder*
. . . round	. . . Spiel *shpeel*

Can I hire . . . ?	Kann ich . . . mieten?
	kan ikh . . . meeten?
I'd like to hire . . .	Ich möchte . . . mieten
	ikn murkhter . . . meeten
Where can I hire . . . ?	Wo kann ich . . . mieten?
	vo kan ikh . . . meeten?

. . . a bicycle	. . . ein Fahrrad . . .
	I-n faarraat
. . . a boat	. . . ein Boot . . .
	I-n boht
. . . equipment	. . . eine Ausrüstung . . .
	I-ner owsrewstoong
. . . a sailboard	. . . einen Windsurfer . . .
	I-nen vintsoorfer

The beach

● The coasts of Germany, facing the North Sea and the
Baltic, have many miles of sandy beaches and dunes.
These can be rather windy, so it is worth hiring a
Strandkorb, a wicker chair with a hood.

Can you recommend a beach?	Können Sie einen Strand empfehlen?
	kurnen zee I-nen shtrant empfailen?
Is it safe for children?	Ist es für Kinder ungefährlich?
	ist es fewr kinder oongerfairlikh?
Is it safe for swimming?	Kann man hier ohne Gefahr schwimmen?
	Kan man heer ohner gerfaar shvimmen?
Is there a lifeguard?	Gibt es eine Strandwache?
	gipt es I-ner shtrant-vakher?

When is high tide/low tide?	**Wann ist Flut/Ebbe?** *van ist floot/ebber?*
I want to hire ...	**Ich möchte ... mieten** *ikh murkhter ... meeten*
... a deck-chair	**... einen Liegestuhl ...** *I-nen leeger-shtool*
... a sailing boat	**... ein Segelboot ...** *I-n saigel-boht*
... a sunshade	**... einen Sonnenschirm ...** *I-nen zonnen-sheerm*
... a surfboard	**... ein Surfbrett ...** *I-n zoorf-bret*

You may hear:

Es ist (nicht) gefährlich *es ist (nikht) gerfairlikh*	It's (not) dangerous

You may see:

Angeln verboten	No fishing
Baden verboten	No swimming
Bootsverleih	Boat hire
Eisstadion	Ice rink
Fahrradverleih	Bicycle hire
Fahrradweg	Cycle path
Freibad	Open-air swimming pool
Gefahr	Danger
Hallenbad	Indoor swimming pool
Lawinengefahr	Danger of avalanches
Privatstrand	Private beach
Tennisplätze	Tennis courts
Zuschauer	Spectators
Zum Skilift	To the skilift

Winter sports

I want to hire . . .	Ich möchte . . . mieten *ikh murkhter . . . meeten*
. . . a complete set of ski equipment	. . . eine komplette Skiausrüstung . . . *I-ner kompletter shee-owsrewstoong*
. . . skis	. . . Skier . . . *shee-er*
. . . ski boots	. . . Skistiefel . . . *shee-shteeferl*
Can I take skiing lessons?	Kann ich Skiunterricht nehmen? *kan ikh shee-oonterikht naimen?*
Are there . . . ?	Gibt es . . . ? *gipt es . . . ?*
. . . ski-runs for beginners	. . . Skipisten für Anfänger *shee-peesten fewr anfenger*
. . . ski-runs for advanced skiers	. . . Skipisten für Fortgeschrittene *sheepeesten fewr fortgershrittener*
. . . ski-lifts	. . . Skilifte *sheelifter*
How much does a daily/weekly lift pass cost?	Was kostet eine Tageskarte/Wochenkarte für den Lift? *vas kostet I-ner taages-karter/vokhen-karter fewr dain lift?*
What are the snow conditions like?	Wie sind die Schneeverhältnisse? *vee sint dee shnai-fairheltnisser?*

- As Germany is in the European Community, UK visitors are entitled to free medical and dental treatment, even if they have no private holiday insurance (which is, in any case, a useful back-up). Full details are given in the booklet which accompanies the E111 form which you get from the DHSS.
- When travelling to either Austria or Switzerland, you will need to take out health insurance.
- Be careful of the sun: it is very easy to forget, especially when it is windy or when skiing. It is usually cheaper to buy sun protection creams before you leave.
- Chemists (*Apotheke*) will give advice – see page 110 – and every town has its duty chemist open all night or at the weekend.
- For emergency telephone numbers, see page 136.

At the doctor's

My ... hurts	... tut mir weh *toot meer vai*
... **arm**	Der Arm ... *dair aarm*
... **back**	Der Rücken ... *dair rewken*
... **chest**	Die Brust ... *dee broost*
... **eye**	Das Auge ... *das owger*
... **head**	Der Kopf ... *dair kopf*
... **leg**	Das Bein ... *das byn*
... **stomach**	Der Magen ... *dair maagen*
... **neck**	Der Hals ... *dair haals*
... **foot**	Der Fuß ... *dair foos*
I've been bitten (animal)	Ich bin gebissen worden *ikh bin gerbissen worden*
I've been stung	Ich bin gestochen worden *ikh bin gerstokhen worden*
He/she is ...	Er/sie ... *air/zee ...*
... **unconscious**	... ist bewußtlos *ist bervoostlohs*
... **bleeding**	... blutet *blootet*
... **seriously injured**	... ist schwer verletzt *ist shvair fairletst*

Health

I've got . . .	Ich habe . . . *ikh haaber . . .*
. . . asthma	. . . Asthma *astma*
. . . a chest pain	. . . Brustschmerzen *broostshmairtsen*
. . . a cold	. . . eine Erkältung *I-ner airkeltoong*
. . . a cough	. . . Husten *hoosten*
. . . earache	. . . Ohrenschmerzen *ohrenshmairtsen*
. . . something in my eye	. . . etwas in meinem Auge *etvas in mynem owger*
. . . hayfever	. . . Heuschnupfen *hoyshnoopfen*
. . . a migraine	. . . Migräne *migrainer*
. . . period pains	. . . Menstruations- beschwerden *menstroo-atsiohns- bershvairden*
. . . a rash	. . . einen Ausschlag *I-nen ows-shlaag*
. . . a sore throat	. . . einen Halsschmerzen *I-nen hals-shmairtsen*
. . . sunstroke	. . . einen Sonnenstich *I-nen zonnen-shtikh*

There's been an accident	Es ist ein Unfall passiert *es ist I-n oonfal passeert*
Can you fetch a doctor?	Können Sie einen Arzt holen? *kurnen zee I-nen aartst hohlen?*

I feel faint/sick	Ich fühle mich schwach/ schlecht
	ikh fewler mikh shvakh/ shlekht
I feel dizzy	Mir ist schwindelig
	meer ist shvinderlig
I've got diarrhoea/a temperature	Ich habe Durchfall/Fieber
	ikh haaber doorkhfal/feeber
I've been sick	Ich habe mich übergeben
	ikh haaber mikh ewbergaiben
It hurts . . .	Es tut weh . . .
	es toot vai . . .
. . . all the time	. . . die ganze Zeit
	dee gantser tsyt
. . . when I do this	. . . wenn ich das mache
	ven ikh das makher

I am . . .	Ich bin . . .
	ikh bin . . .

. . . diabetic	. . . Diabetiker
	diabaitiker
. . . epileptic	. . . Epileptiker
	Epileptikker
. . . pregnant	. . . schwanger
	shvanger
. . . allergic to antibiotics/ penicillin	. . . allergisch gegen Antibiotika/Penizillin
	alairgish gaigen antibiohtika/penitsileen

I'm on the Pill	Ich nehme die Pille
	ikh naimer dee piller
I had a heart attack	Ich hatte einen Herzinfarkt
	ikh hatter I-nen hairtsinfaarkt
I need a prescription for . . .	Ich brauche ein Rezept für . . .
	ikh browkher I-n retsept fewr

Is it serious?

Ist es schlimm?
ist es shlim?

Could you tell my family/ hotel?

Können Sie bitte meine Familie/mein Hotel benachrichtigen?
kurnen zee bitter myner fameelier/myn hotel bernakhrikhtigen?

You may hear:

Ich gebe Ihnen . . .
ikh gaiber eenen

I'll give you . . .

. . . eine Spritze
I-ner shpritser

. . . an injection

. . . eine Salbe
I-ner zalber

. . . some ointment

. . . ein Rezept
I-n retsept

. . . a prescription

. . . ein Schmerzmittel
I-n shmairtsmittel

. . . a painkiller

Wo tut es weh?
voh toot es vai?

Where does it hurt?

Wie lange geht es Ihnen schon so?
vee langer gait es eenen shohn zo?

How long have you been feeling like this?

Tief atmen, bitte
teef aatmen bitter

Breathe deeply, please

Husten Sie, bitte
hoosten zee bitter

Cough, please

Sie müssen . . . Tage lang im Bett bleiben
zee mewssen . . . taager lang im bet blyben

You must stay in bed for . . . days

Sie müssen ins Krankenhaus gehen
zee mewssen ins krankenhows gai-en

You must go to hospital

I've been in pain . . .	Das habe ich seit . . . *das haaber ikh zyt*
. . . for several days	. . . einigen Tagen *I-nigen taagen*
. . . since yesterday	. . . gestern *gestern*
. . . since this morning	. . . heute morgen *hoyter morgen*
. . . for a few hours	. . . einigen Stunden *I-nigen shtoonden*
May I have a receipt for my insurance company?	Kann ich eine Quittung für meine Krankenkasse haben? *kan ikh I-ner kvittoong fewr myner kranken-kasser haaben?*
May I have a medical certificate?	Kann ich einen Krankenschein haben? *kan ikh I-nen kranken-shyn haaben?*
Could you sign this please?	Können Sie das bitte unterschreiben? *kurnen zee das bitter oonter-shryben?*

You may see:

Alle Kassen	All health insurance patients
Arzt/Ärztin für Allgemeinmedizin	General Practitioner
Facharzt/fachärztin für . . . Krankheiten	Specialist in . . .
Krankenhaus/Klinik	Hospital
Krankenwagen	ambulance
Nach Vereinbarung	By appointment
Notarzt	Emergency Doctor

What's wrong?

You may hear:

Es ist . . . *es ist . . .*	It's . . .
. . . eine **Blinddarmentzündung** *I-ner blintdarment-tsewndoong*	. . . appendicitis
. . . eine **Gehirnerschütterung** *I-ner gerheern-ershewtteroong*	. . . concussion
. . . eine **Grippe** *I-ner gripper*	. . . flu
. . . eine **Lebensmittelvergiftung** *I-ner laibenzmittel-fairgiftoong*	. . . food poisoning
. . . eine **Magenverstimmung** *I-ner maagen-fairshtimmoong*	. . . a stomach upset
. . . ein **Sonnenstich** *I-n zonnen-shtikh*	. . . sunstroke
. . . **gebrochen** *gerbrokhen*	. . . broken/fractured
. . . **infiziert** *infitseert*	. . . infected
. . . **verrenkt** *fairrenkt*	. . . dislocated
. . . **verstaucht** *fairshtowkht*	. . . sprained

At the dentist's

I've got toothache	Ich habe Zahnschmerzen *ikh haaber tsaan-shmairtsen*
Can you recommend a dentist?	Können Sie einen Zahnarzt empfehlen? *kurnen zee I-nen tsaan-artst empfailen?*
Can I make an appointment?	Kann ich einen Termin haben? *kan ikh ynen tairmeen haaben?*
It's urgent	Es ist dringend *es ist dringent*
I've lost a filling/crown	Ich habe eine Plombe verloren *ikh haaber I-ner plomber fairloren*
It's this tooth	Es ist dieser Zahn *es ist deezer tsaan*
Can you give me an anaesthetic?	Können Sie mir eine Spritze geben? *kurnen zee meer I-ner shpritzer gaiben?*
I've broken my denture	Ich habe meine Prothese zerbrochen *ikh haaber myner prohtaizer zerbrokhen*
Can you repair it?	Können Sie es reparieren? *kurnen zee es repareeren?*
How long will it take?	Wie lange dauert es? *vee langer dowert es?*
I'm insured	Ich bin versichert *ikh bin fairsikhert*

You may hear:

Welcher Zahn tut Ihnen weh? *velkher tsaan toot eenen vai?*	Which tooth hurts?

Road

- **Motorways (expressways):** *Autobahnen* in Germany do not charge tolls, but a toll (*die Maut/die Gebühr*) is payable on some mountain roads and tunnels in Austria, and in Switzerland you must display a special sticker (*die Vignette*), available in Britain from the AA or RAC.
- **Speed limits:**

motorways	no speed limit for cars
built-up areas	50 km/h (30 mph)
other roads	100 km/h (60 mph)

- **Right of way:** traffic coming from the right has priority at junctions, unless it is entering from, for example, a service road, or there is a priority sign (a yellow diamond, or an arrow in a triangle).
- You should obtain a green card from your insurance company before taking your car abroad. Additional breakdown policies are also available. For full details contact the AA or RAC.

How do I get to (+ place name)/to (+ building, street) . . . ?	Wie komme ich nach/zu . . . ? *vee kommer ikh nakh/tsoo . . . ?*
How far is it to (+ place name)/to (+ building, road) . . . ?	Wie weit ist es nach/zu . . . ? *vee vyt ist es nakh/tsoo . . . ?*
How long does it take?	Wie lange dauert es? *vee langer dowert es?*
Am I on the right road for . . . ?	Bin ich auf der richtigen Straße nach . . . ? *bin ikh owf dair rikhtigen shtraaser nakh . . . ?*
Can you show it to me on the map/on the street map?	Können Sie es mir auf der Karte/auf dem Stadtplan zeigen? *kurnen zee es meer owf dair karter/owf dem shtatplaan tsygen?*
Where can I park?	Wo kann ich parken? *vo kan ikh parken?*

You may hear:

Nehmen Sie die Straße nach/über . . . *naimen zee dee shtraaser nakh/ewber . . .*	Take the road for/via . . .
Fahren Sie Richtung . . . *faaren zee rikhtoong . . .*	Go in the direction of . . .
Sie sind auf der falschen Straße *zee zint owf dair falshen shtraaser*	You're on the wrong road
Sie müssen zurück nach . . . *zee mewssen tsoorewk nakh . . .*	You'll have to go back to . . .
nördlich/südlich von . . . *nurdlikh/sewdlikh fon . . .*	to the north/south of . . .
östlich/westlich von . . . *urstlikh/vestlikh fon . . .*	to the east/west of . . .

Travel

Fahren Sie ... *faaren zee ...*	Go ...
... geradeaus *geraaderows*	... straight on
... nach links *nakh links*	... left
... nach rechts *nakh rekhts*	... right

... bis zur ersten/zweiten
  Kreuzung
  bis tsoor airsten/tsvyten
  Kroytsoong
	... to the first/second
	  junction

... bis zur Ampel *bis tsoor ampel*	... to the traffic lights

Filling Station/Garage

• Many filling stations in Germany are self-service
(*Selbstbedienung*, or *SB* for short). Lead-free petrol is
available everywhere.

Where's the nearest filling station/garage?	Wo ist die nächste Tankstelle/ Reparaturwerkstatt? *vo ist dee nekhste* *tankshteller/* *reparatoorverkshtat?*
Please fill the tank	Volltanken, bitte *foltanken, bitter*
4 star (premium)	Super *zooper*
2 star	Normal *normaal*
lead-free	bleifrei *blyfry*
diesel	Diesel *deesel*

75

Please check/charge/repair ...	Bitte überprüfen/wechseln/reparieren Sie ...
	bitter ewberprewfen/vekhzeln/repareeren zee ...
... the oil	... das Öl
	das url
... the water	... das Kühlwasser
	das kewlvasser
... the brake fluid	... die Bremsflüssigkeit
	dee bremsflewsigkyt
... the tyres	... die Reifen
	dee ryfen
... the spare tyre	... den Ersatzreifen
	dain erzatsryfen
... the battery	... die Batterie
	dee bateree
... the bulb	... die Glühbirne
	dee glewbirner
... the fanbelt	... den Keilriemen
	dain kylreemen
... the fuse	... die Sicherung
	dee zikheroong
... the spark(ing) plugs	... die Zündkerzen
	dee tsewnt-kairtsen
... the tyre	... den Reifen
	dain ryfen
... the windscreen (windshield)	... die Windschutzscheibe
	dee vintshoots-shyber
... the brakes	... die Bremsen
	dee bremzen
... the exhaust pipe	... den Auspuff
	dain owspoof
... the radiator	... den Kühler
	dain kewler

Breakdown

Where's the nearest garage?	Wo ist die nächste Reparaturwerkstatt? *voh ist dee nekhster reparatoor-vairkshtat?*
I've had a breakdown	Ich habe eine Panne *ikh haaber I-ner panner*
I've got a flat tyre	Ich habe einen Platten *ikh haaber I-nen platten*
I've run out of petrol (gas)	Mir ist das Benzin ausgegangen *meer ist das bentseen ows-gergangen*
The engine won't start	Der Motor springt nicht an *dair motor shpringt nikht an*
The engine is overheating	Der Motor läuft heiß *dair mohtor loyft hys*
The battery is flat	Die Batterie ist leer *dee bateree ist lair*
There's something wrong with the . . .	. . . ist nicht in Ordnung *. . . ist nikht in ordnoong*
Please send a mechanic/a breakdown truck	Bitte schicken Sie einen Mechaniker/einen Abschleppwagen *bitter shikken zee I-nen mekaaniker/I-nen abshlepvaagen*
I'm on the road from . . . to . . .	Ich bin auf der Straße zwischen . . . und . . . *ikh bin owf dair shtraasser tsvishen . . . oont . . .*
I'm 5 kilometers from . . .	Ich bin fünf Kilometer von . . . *ikh bin fewnf kilomaiter fon . . .*
How long will it take?	Wie lange dauert es? *vee langer dowert es?*

● See page 131 for numbers.

Accident

- For emergency numbers, see page 136.

There's been an accident	Es ist ein Unfall passiert *es ist I-n oonfal paseert*
on the road from . . . to . . .	auf der Straße zwischen . . . und . . . *owf dair shtraasser tsvishen . . . oont . . .*
about 4 km from . . .	ungefähr vier Kilometer von . . . *oon-gefair feer kilomaiter fon . . .*
Where's the nearest phone?	Wo ist das nächste Telefon? *vo ist das nekhster telefohn?*
Please call the police	Rufen Sie bitte die Polizei *roofen zee bitter dee polits-I*
Call a doctor quickly	Rufen Sie schnell einen Arzt *roofen zee shnell I-nen aartst*
There are people injured	Es hat Verletzte gegeben *es hat fairletster gergaiben*
Police	Polizei *polits-I*
Ambulance	Krankenwagen *krankenvaagen*
My/your registration number	meine/Ihre Autonummer *myner/eerer owtoh-noomer*
My/your name	mein/Ihr Name *myn/eer naamer*
my/your address	meine/Ihre Adresse *myner/eerer adresser*
My/your driving licence	mein/Ihr Führerschein *myn/eer fewrer-shyn*
my/your insurance company	meine/Ihre Versicherungsgesellschaft *myner/eerer fairsikheroongs-gerselshaft*

You may see:

- Most roadsigns are identical to those found in Britain.
- The words and phrases listed below are commonly found on roadsigns and notices.

Anliegerverkehr frei ⎫ Nur für Anlieger ⎭	access to residents/owners only
Ausfahrt	exit
Bahnübergang	railway crossing
Baustelle	roadworks
Durchgangsverkehr	through traffic
Einbahnstraße	one-way street
Einordnen	get in lane
Fahrradweg	cycle path
Fußgängerzone	pedestrian zone
Gefährliche Kurve	dangerous bend
Gegenverkehr	two-way traffic
Gesperrt für Fahrzeuge	closed to vehicles
Glatteis	black ice
Halteverbot	no stopping
Kriechspur	slow lane
Langsam fahren	slow
Lkw	lorry/truck
Nicht überholen	no overtaking
Parkplatz	car-park/parking lot
Parkscheibe/Parkuhren	parking disc/parking meters
Pkw	car
Raststätte	services
Überholen verboten	no overtaking
Umleitung	diversion
... Verboten	no ...
Vorsicht	caution

Buying a ticket

When is the next . . . to Bonn?	Wann ist der nächste . . . nach Bonn? *van ist dair nekhster . . . nakh bon?*
. . . flight	. . . Flug . . . *floog*
. . . train	. . . Zug . . . *tsoog*
. . . bus/coach	. . . Bus . . . *boos*
When does it arrive?	Wann kommt er an? *van komt air an?*
Do I have to change?	Muß ich umsteigen? *moos ikh oomshtygen?*

I'd like a . . . ticket to Bonn	Ich möchte eine Fahrkarte nach Bonn . . . *ikh murkhter I-ner faarkaarter nakh bon . . .*
. . . single (one way)	. . . einfach *I-nfakh*
. . . return	. . . hin und zurück *hin oont zoorewk*
. . . first class	. . . erste Klasse *airster klasser*
. . . second class	. . . zweite Klasse *tsvyter klasser*

I'd like to book a seat/berth	Ich möchte einen Platz/einen Platz im Schlafwagen reservieren lassen *ikh murkhter I-nen plats/I-nen platz im shlaafvaagen rezairveeren lassen*
What does it cost?	Was kostet es? *vas kostet es?*

Plane

Is it a direct flight?	Ist es ein Direktflug? *ist es I-n direktfloog?*
Is there a connection to Munich?	Gibt es einen Anschluß nach München? *gipt es I-nen an-shloos nakh mewnchen?*
When does the plane take off?	Wann ist der Abflug? *van ist dair abfloog?*
When do we land?	Wann landen wir? *van landen veer?*
What is the flight number?	Welche Flugnummer ist es? *velkher floog-noomer ist es?*
When must I check in?	Wann muß ikh einchecken? *van moos ikh I-ncheken?*
Is there an airport bus?	Gibt es einen Flughafenbus? *gipt es I-nen flooghaafenboos?*
I'd like to . . . my reservation	Ich murkhter meine Reservierung . . . *ikh murkhter myner rezerveeroong . . .*
. . . confirm	. . . bestätigen *bershtaitigen*
. . . alter	. . . umbuchen *oombookhen*
. . . cancel	. . . annullieren *anooleeren*

You may see:	
Abflug	Departure
Ankunft	Arrival
Ausland	International (flights)
Fluggäste	Passengers
Inland	Internal (flights)

Rail

- The main types of train are:
  - **TEE-Zug**: Trans European Express (1st class only – supplement [*Zuschlag*] payable)
  - **IC-Zug**: Inter-City (often 1st class only – supplement payable)
  - **D-Zug**: Express (supplement payable for journeys under 50 km) (*Städteschnellzug* in Austria, *Schnellzug* in Austria, Switzerland)
  - **E-Zug**: Moderately fast train – does not stop at small stations
  - **N-Zug**: Local train, stopping at all stations (*Personenzug* in Austria, *Regionalzug* in Switzerland)
- Coaches on long-distance international trains are often regrouped along their route for different destinations. It is important to get on the right *Kurswagen* by checking the destination plate on the coaches; you can find the approximate position of the coach beforehand by looking at the *Wagenstandanzeiger* on the platform.
- Remember that German railway stations show two timetables:

    Abfahrt Departures   *Ankunft* Arrivals
- Other useful terms are:
  - **Speisewagen** Dining car
  - **Schlafwagen** Sleeping car with compartments containing a washbasin and one, two or three berths
  - **Liegewagen** Coach containing berths with sheets, blankets and pillows. Cheaper than the *Schlafwagen*.
- It is advisable to reserve your seat or berth in advance.
- If you do not have the time to buy a ticket before boarding the train, you may buy one from the guard (*Schaffner*) on the train, as long as you go to find him as soon as possible.

At the Station

Where is/are the . . . ?	Wo ist/sind . . . ? *voh ist/zint . . . ?*
. . . (currency) exchange office	. . . die Wechselstube *dee vekhsel-shtoober*
. . . left-luggage counter (baggage check)	. . . die Gepäckaufbewahrung *dee gerpeck-owfbervaaroong*
. . . lost property office	. . . das Fundbüro *das foont-bewroh*
. . . luggage check-in	. . . die Gepäckaufgabe *dee gerpeck-owfgaaber*
. . . luggage check-out	. . . die Gerpäckausgabe *dee gerpeck-owsgaaber*
. . . newsstand	. . . das Zeitungskiosk *das tsytoongs-kee-osk*
. . . platform 2	. . . Gleis 2/Bahnsteig 2 *glys tsvy/baan-shtyg tsvy*
. . . reservations office	. . . die Platzreservierung *dee plats-rezerveeroong*
. . . restaurant	. . . das Restaurant *das restauron*
. . . snack bar	. . . der Schnellimbiß *dair shnel-imbis*
. . . ticket office/counter	. . . der Fahrkartenschalter *dair faar-kaarten-shalter*
. . . waiting room	. . . der Wartesaal *dair vaarter-zaal*
. . . the toilets	. . . die Toiletten *dee twaletten*
. . . luggage-lockers	. . . die Schließfächer *dee shlees-fekher*
. . . luggage-trolleys	. . . die Kofferkulis *dee koffer-koolis*

83

You may see:

Abfahrt	Departure
Ankunft	Arrival
Ausgang	Exit
Auskunft	Information
Eingang	Entrance
Zu den Gleisen **Zu den Zügen**	To the platforms
Hauptbahnhof (Hbf)	Main station
Kurswagen	Through coach
Nichtraucher	Non-smoker (compartment)
Raucher	Smoker (compartment)
Wagenstandanzeiger	Order of cars (See introductory note on page 82)

I'd like to reserve . . .	Ich möchte . . . reservieren *ikh murkhter . . . rezerveeren*
. . . a seat/2 seats	. . . einen Platz/zwei Plätz *I-nen plats/tsvy pletser*
. . . by the window	. . . am Fenster *am fenster*
. . . in a no-smoking compartment	. . . in einem Nichtraucherabteil *in I-nem nikht-rowkher-abtyl*
. . . in a smoking compartment	. . . in einem Raucherabteil *in I-nem rowkherabtyl*
. . . a berth in the sleeping car	. . . einen Platz im Schlafwagen *I-nen plats im shlaafvaagen*

Do I have to pay a surcharge?	Muß ich einen Zuschlag bezahlen? *moos ikh I-nen tsoo-shlaag bertsaalen?*
Will the train leave on time?	Fährt der Zug pünktlich ab? *fairt dair tsoog pewnktlikh ap?*
Will the train arrive on time?	Kommt der Zug pünktlich an? *komt dair tsoog pewnktlikh an?*
Is there enough time to change?	Reicht die Zeit zum Umsteigen? *rykht dee tsyt tsoom oom-shtygen?*
Does the train stop in Bonn?	Hält der Zug in Bonn? *helt dair tsoog in bon?*
What platform does the train to Bonn leave from?	Auf welchem Gleis fährt der Zug nach Bonn ab? *owf velkhem glys fairt dair tsoog nakh bon ap?*
Does the train have a restaurant car/a sleeping-car?	Führt der Zug einen Speisewagen/einen Schlafwagen? *fewrt dair tsoog I-nen shpyser-vaagen/I-nen shlaaf-vaagen?*
Is this the train to Bonn?	Ist das der Zug nach Bonn? *ist das dair tsoog nakh bon?*
I'd like to leave my luggage	Ich möchte mein Gepäck einstellen *ikh murkhte myn gerpeck I-nshtelen*
I'd like to register (check) my luggage	Ich möchte mein Gepäck aufgeben *ikh murkhter myn gerpeck owfgaiben*

On the Train

Is this seat free?	Ist dieser Platz frei? *ist deezer plats fry?*
This seat's taken	Dieser Platz ist besetzt *deezer plats ist berzetst*
I think this is my seat	Ich glaube, das ist mein Platz *ikh glowber das ist myn plats*
Excuse me. May I come past?	Entschuldigung. Kann ich vorbei? *ent-shooldigoong kan ikh forby?*
What station is this?	Wie heißt dieser Ort? *vee hyst deezer ort?*
How long will the train stop here?	Wie lange hält der Zug hier? *vee lange helt dair tsoog heer?*
Where is my berth?	Wo ist meine Kabine? *voh ist myner kabeener?*
Please wake me at 6	Bitte wecken Sie mich um 6 Uhr *bitte veken zee mikh um zekhs oor*
Would you bring me coffee at 6?	Würden Sie mir bitte um 6 Uhr Kaffee bringen? *vewrden zee meer bitter oom zekhs oor kafai bringen?*

You may hear:

Es fährt einen Zug nach Bonn um . . . *es fairt I-nen tsoog nakh bon oom . . .*	There's a train to Bonn at . . .
Steigen Sie in . . . um *shtygen zee in . . . oom*	Change in . . .

Der Fahrkartenschalter ist . . . *dair faarkartenshalter ist . . .*	The ticket office is . . .
. . . da drüben *da drewben*	. . . over there
. . . links *links*	. . . on the left
. . . rechts *rekhts*	. . . on the right
. . . oben *ohben*	. . . upstairs
. . . unten *oonten*	. . . downstairs
Der Zug hat . . . Minuten Verspätung *dair tsoog hat . . . minooten fairshpaitoong*	The train will be . . . minutes late
Erste Klasse . . . des Zuges *airster klaser . . . des tsooges*	First class . . . of the train
. . . an der Spitze *an dair shpitse*	. . . at the front
. . . in der Mitte *in dair mitter*	. . . in the middle
. . . am Ende *am ender*	. . . at the end

Can you tell me when we get to . . . ?	Sagen Sie mir bitte wenn wir in . . . ankommen *zaagen zee meer bitter ven veer in . . . ankommen*

● For taxis, see page 12.

You may see or hear:

Achtung! *akhtoong*	Attention/watch out!
aussteigen *ows-shtygen*	to get off/out
Bahnsteigkarte *baanshtygkaarter*	platform ticket
einsteigen *I-nshtygen*	to get in/on
Nichtraucher *nikht-rowkher*	non-smoker
Notbremse *nohtbremzer*	emergency cord
planmäßig *planmesig*	scheduled
Platzkarte *platskarter*	seat reservation
Raucher *rowkher*	smoker
sonn- und feiertags *zon oont fyertaagz*	Sundays and holidays
Strecke *shtreker*	route
verkehrt nicht an . . . *fairkairt nikht an . . .*	does not run on . . . (days)
verkehrt nur an . . . *fairkairt noor an . . .*	runs only on . . . (days)
Zug fährt sofort ab! *tsoog fairt zofort ab!*	train now leaving!
zurücktreten! *tsoorewk-traiten!*	stand clear!
zuschlagpflichtig *tsooshlag-pflikhtig*	subject to supplementary fare (see note at head of section)

Bus, Tram and Underground

- Automatic ticket dispensers are found in many cities. If you intend to make a number of journeys, it may be worth your while to buy a booklet of tickets.
- Tickets must usually be passed through an automatic stamping machine (*Entwerter*) as you get on the bus, tram or underground (subway).

I'd like a book of tickets	Ich möchte ein Fahrscheinheft *ikh murkhter I-n faarshynheft*
Where is the . . . ?	Wo ist . . . ? *voh ist . . . ?*
. . . bus-stop	. . . die Haltestelle *dee haltershtelle*
. . . bus-station	. . . der Busbahnhof *dair boosbaanhohf*
. . . station	. . . die Station *dee statsyohn*
Does this bus stop in . . . ?	Hält dieser Bus in . . . ? *helt deezer boos in . . . ?*
Can you tell me where to get off, please?	Können Sie mir bitte sagen, wo ich aussteigen muß? *kurnen zee meer bitter zaagen voh ikh ows-shtygen moos?*
I'd like to get off here	Ich möchte hier aussteigen *ikh murkhter ows-shtygen*

You may hear:

Nehmen Sie Bus Linie 6 *naimen zee boos leenyer zekhs*	Take a number 6
Ein Bus fährt alle 10 Minuten *I-n boos fairt aller tsain minooten*	A bus leaves every 10 minutes

Does this bus go to . . . ?	Fährt dieser Bus . . . ? *fairt deezer boos . . . ?*
Which bus goes to . . . ?	Welcher Bus fährt . . . ? *velkher boos fairt . . . ?*
How often are the buses to . . . ?	Wie oft fahren die Büsse . . . ? *vee oft faaren dee bewser . . . ?*
How many stops to . . . ?	Wieviele Haltestellen sind es bis . . . ? *veefeeler haltershtellen zint es bis . . . ?*

. . . the cathedral	. . . zum Dom *tsoom dohm*
. . . the museum	. . . zum Museum *tsoom moozai-oom*
. . . the Old Town	. . . zur Altstadt *tsoor altshtat*
. . . the theatre	. . . zum Theater *tsoom tai-aater*
. . . the Youth Hostel	. . . zur Jugendherberge *tsoor yoogenthairbairger*
. . . Würzburg	. . . nach Würzburg *nakh vewrtsboorg*

When is the next bus to . . . ?	Wann fährt der nächste Bus nach . . . ? *van fairt dair nekhster boos nakh . . . ?*
How much is the fare to . . . ?	Was kostet es nach . . . ? *vas kostet es nakh . . . ?*

You may see:	
Bushaltestelle	regular bus stop
Bedarfshaltestelle	stops on request

● For directions, see page 74.

Boats and ferries

When is there a boat for . . . ?	Wann fährt ein Schiff nach . . . ? *van fairt I-n shif nakh . . . ?*
Where does it leave from?	Wo fährt es ab? *voh fairt es ap?*
When do we call in . . . ?	Wann legen wir in . . . an? *van laigen veer in . . . an?*
How long does the crossing last?	Wie lange dauert die Überfahrt? *vee langer dowert dee ewberfaart?*
We'd like a trip on the river	Wir möchten eine Flußfahrt machen *veer murkhten I-ner floosfaart makhen*
We'd like a cabin	Wir möchten eine Kabine *veer murkhten I-ner kabeener*
There's . . .	Wir sind . . . *veer zint . . .*
. . . 1 adult/2 adults	. . . ein Erwachsener/zwei Erwachsene *I-n airvakhsener/tsvy airvakhsener*
. . . 1 child/2 children	. . . ein Kind/zwei Kinder *I-n kint/tsvy kinnder*
We have . . .	Wir haben . . . *veer haaben . . .*
. . . a car	. . . ein Auto *I-n owtoh*
. . . bicycles	. . . Fahrräder *faar-raider*
. . . a caravan	. . . einen Wohnwagen *I-nen vohn-vaagen*
. . . a motorbike	. . . ein Motorrad *I-n motohr-raat*

Sightseeing

- Most towns have a tourist information office, signposted with a large latter 'i'. They can help with information not only about places of interest and events, but also accommodation.

Where's the information office?	Wo ist das Informationsbüro? *vo ist das informatsyohns-bewroh?*
What are the main places of interest?	Was sind die Hauptsehenswürdigkeiten? *vas zint dee howpt-zaiens-vewrdikh-kyten?*
What is there of interest to children?	Was ist für Kinder interessant? *vas ist fewr kinnder interessant?*

Where is/are the . . . ?	Wo ist/sind . . . ? *vo ist/zint . . . ?*
. . . art gallery	. . . die Kunstgalerie *dee koonstgalleree*
. . . castle	. . . das Schloß/die Burg *das shlos/dee boorg*
. . . cathedral	. . . die Kathedrale/der Dom *dee katadraaler/dair dohm*
. . . concert hall	. . . die Konzerthalle *dee kontsairt-haller*
. . . conference centre	. . . die Kongreßhalle *dee kongress-haller*
. . . exhibition centre	. . . das Messegelände *das messer-gerlender*
. . . town centre	. . . die Innenstadt *dee innenshtat*

Is the . . . worth visiting?	Ist . . . sehenswert? *ist . . . zai-enzvairt?*
Have we got time to visit . . . ?	Haben wir noch Zeit, . . . zu besichtigen? *haaben veer nokh tsyt, . . . tsoo berzikhtigen?*
I'm interested in . . .	Ich interessiere mich für . . . *ikh interesseerer mikh fewr . . .*
. . . archaeology	. . . Archäologie *arkh-eh-ologee*
. . . art	. . . Kunst *koonst*
. . . history	. . . Geschichte *ger-shikhter*
. . . music	. . . Musik *moozeek*
. . . natural history	. . . Naturkunde *natoor-koonder*
. . . technology	. . . Technik *tekhnik*

Admission

- Most museums, galleries and places of interest in Germany are closed on Mondays.

Is it open on Saturdays/ today/tomorrow?	Ist es samstags/heute/morgen geöffnet? *ist es zamztaagz/hoyter/ morgen ger-urfnet?*
What are the opening times?	Was sind die öffnungszeiten? *vas zint dee urfnoongz-tsyten?*
There are four of us	Wir sind 4 Personen *veer zint feer pairzohnen*

93

2 adults/children	2 Erwachsene/Kinder *tsvy airvakhsener/kinnder*
I'd like a guide book (in English)	Ich möchte einen Reiseführer (in English) *ikh murkhter I-nen ryzer-fewrer (in ennglish)*
When does it close?	Wann schließt es? *van shleest es?*
How much is the entrance fee?	Was kostet der Eintritt? *vas kostet dair I-ntritt?*
Can I take photographs?	Darf man fotografieren? *darf man fohtografeeren?*
Are there special rates for . . . ?	Gibt es Ermäßigungen für . . . ? *gipt es air-maissigoongen fewr . . . ?*
. . . children	. . . Kinder *kinnder*
. . . disabled people	. . . Behinderte *ber-hinnderter*
. . . groups	. . . Gruppen *groopen*
. . . pensioners	. . . Rentner *rentner*
. . . students	. . . Studenten *shtoodenten*

You may see:	
Eintrittspreise	Admission charges
Eintritt frei	Admission free
Fotografieren verboten Fotografieren nicht gestattet	No photography
Rauchen verboten	No smoking

In the country

- The countryside and forests are crisscrossed with large numbers of well-marked footpaths (*Wanderwege*). A map showing the footpaths in the locality (*eine Wanderkarte*) will help you to get the best out of these.
- In mountain areas, signposts show distances in hours rather than kilometres.

How far is it to ... ?	Wie weit ist es nach ... ? *vee vyt ist es nakh ... ?*
How long will it take?	Wie lange dauert es? *vee langer dowert es?*
How do I get to ... ?	Wie komme ich nach ... ? *vee kommer ikh nakh ... ?*
Is there a pub near here?	Ist ein Gasthaus in der Nähe? *ist I-n gast-hows in dair nai-er?*
Where does this footpath/road lead to?	Wohin führt dieser Fußweg/diese Straße? *voh-hin fewrt deezer foossvaig/deezer shtraasser?*

What's the name of this ... ?	Wie heißt ... ? *vee hysst ... ?*
... castle	... das Schloß *das shloss*
... lake	... der See *dair zai*
... river	... der Fluß *dair flooss*
... village	... das Dorf *das dorf*
What's that called in German?	Wie heißt das auf Deutsch? *vee hysst das owf doych?*

Describing Things and Places

It's . . .	Es ist . . . *es ist . . .*
. . . amazing	. . . erstaunlich *air-shtownlikh*
. . . awful	. . . schrecklich *shreklikh*
. . . beautiful	. . . schön *shurn*
. . . boring	. . . langweilig *langvylig*
. . . depressing	. . . deprimierend *deprimeerent*
. . . impressive	. . . beeindruckend *ber-I-ndrookent*
. . . interesting	. . . interessant *interessant*
. . . lovely	. . . wunderschön *voondershurn*
. . . picturesque	. . . malerisch *maalerish*
. . . pretty	. . . hübsch *hewpsh*
. . . romantic	. . . romantisch *rohmantish*
. . . terrible	. . . schrecklich *shreklikh*
. . . strange	. . . seltsam *zeeltzaam*
. . . ugly	. . . häßlich *hesslikh*

I (don't) like it	Es gefällt mir (nicht) *es gerfelt meer (nikht)*

- Opening times are as follows:

	weekdays	Saturdays
Germany	8/9am to 6/6.30pm	8/9am to 12/2pm
Austria	8/9am to 6/6.30pm	8/9am to 12/2pm
Switzerland	8/9am to 6/6.30pm	8/9am to 4/5pm

- Some shops close for lunch.
- In Germany, shops stay open until 6pm on the first Saturday of every month.
- In Switzerland, shops are often closed on Monday morning.
- Bookshops and stationers are usually separate. Magazines and newspapers can be bought at newsstands.
- Chemist's (*Apotheke*) sell only medicines and health items. For toiletries, films etc, look for a *Drogerie*.
- Electricity is 200V, 50 cycle AC almost everywhere is Germany, Austria and Switzerland.

I'm looking for . . .	Ich suche . . . *ikh sookher*
I'm just looking	Ich sehe mich nur um *ikh sai-er mikh noor oom*
Can you help me?	Können Sie mir helfen? *kurnen zee meer helfen?*
Do you have any . . . ?	Haben Sie . . . ? *haaben zee . . . ?*
Where's the . . . department?	Wo ist die . . .-abteilung? *voh ist dee . . . aptyloong?*
Where is the . . . ?	Wo ist . . . ? *voh ist . . . ?*
. . . lift (elevator)	. . . der Fahrstuhl *dair faarshtool*
. . . escalator	. . . die Rolltreppe *dee rol-trepper*
Where are the . . . ?	Wo sind die . . . ? *voh zint dee . . . ?*
I saw it in the window	Ich habe es im Fenster gesehen *ikh haaber es im fenster gersaien*
That one/those	Das da/die da *das daa/dee daa*
Do you have any others?	Haben Sie andere? *haaben zee anderer?*
Do you have any more?	Haben Sie noch mehr davon? *haaben zee nokh mair daafon?*
Do you have it in any other colours?	Haben Sie es in anderen Farben? *haaben zee es in anderen faarben?*
It's for a present	Es ist ein Geschenk *es ist I-n gershenk*

I'm looking for something (a bit) . . .	Ich such etwas (ein bißchen) . . . *ikh sookher etvas (I-n bisskhen) . . .*
. . . cheaper	. . . Billigeres *billigeres*
. . . better	. . . Besseres *besseres*
. . . darker	. . . Dunkleres *doonkleres*
. . . lighter (colour)	. . . Helleres *helleres*
. . . larger	. . . Größeres *grursseres*
. . . smaller	. . . Kleineres *klyneres*
I may come back later	Ich komme vielleicht später zurück *ikh kommer feelykht shpaiter tsoorewk*
I (don't) like it	Es gefallt mir (nicht) *es gerfelt meer (nikht)*
May I try it/them on?	Darf ich es/sie anprobieren? *darf ikh es/zee anprobeeren?*
I'll take it/them	Ich nehme es/sie *ikh naimer es/zee*
I prefer that one	Ich habe lieber dieser *ikh haaber leeber deezer*
Will you gift wrap it, please?	Können Sie es als Geschenk einpacken, bitte? *kurnen zee es als gershenk I-npaken bitter?*
It's not what I'm looking for	Es ist nicht das, was ich suche *es ist nikht das, vas ikh zookher*

Paying

Where is the till/check-out?	Wo ist die Kasse? *voh ist dee kasser?*
How much is it?	Wieviel kostet es? *veefeel kostet es?*
Do you take credit cards/ traveller's cheques?	Nehmen Sie Kreditkarten/ Reiseschecks? *naimen zee kredeetkarten/ ryzer-sheks?*
Must I pay VAT?	Muß ich Mehrwertsteuer bezahlen? *mooss ikh mairvairtshtoyer bertsaalen?*
Can you order it for me?	Können Sie es mir bitte bestellen? *kurnen zee es meer bitter berstellen?*
Can you send it to this address?	Können Sie es an diese Adresse schicken? *kurnen zee es an deezer adresser shiken*
Can you deliver it?	Können Sie es liefern? *kurnen zee es leefern?*
How long will it take?	Wie lange dauert es? *vee langer dowert es?*

You may hear:

Kann ich Ihnen helfen? *kan ikh eenen helfen?*	Can I help you?
Möchten Sie es/sie anprobieren? *murkhten zee es/zee anprobeeren?*	Would you like to try it/ them on?
Welche Farbe/Größe möchten Sie? *velkher faarber/grursser murkhten zee?*	Which colour/size would you like?

Problems

I think you've made a mistake (on the bill)	Ich glaube, Sie haben sich verrechnet *ikh glowber, zee haaben zikh fairrekhnet*
I'd like to exchange this	Ich möchte das umtauschen *ikh murkhter das oomtowshen*
It's ...	Es ist ... *es ist ...*
... the wrong size	... die falsche Größe *dee falsher grursser*
... faulty	... fehlerhaft *failerhaft*
I'd like a refund	Ich möchte mein Geld zurückhaben *ikh murkhter myn gelt tsoorewkhaaben*
Here's the receipt	Hier ist die Quittung *heer ist dee kvitoong*
I bought it yesterday	Ich habe es gestern gekauft *ikh haaber es gestern gerkowft*
It was a present	Es war ein Geschenk *es war I-n gershenk*

You may see:	
Ausgang	Exit
Ausverkauf	Sale
Eingang	Entrance
(Schnell) kasse	(Fast) till/check-out
Selbstbedienung	Self-service
Sonderangebot	Special offer

Shops

Where's the . . . ?	Wo ist . . . ? *voh ist . . . ?*
. . . **baker's**	. . . die Bäckerei *dee beker-I*
. . . **bank**	. . . die Bank *dee Bank*
. . . **butcher's**	. . . die Metzgerei *dee metsger-I*
. . . **camera shop**	. . . das Fotogeschäft *das fohtogersheft*
. . . **chemist's**	. . . die Apotheke *dee apotaiker*
. . . **dry cleaner's**	. . . die chemische Reinigung *dee kaimisher rynigoong*
. . . **greengrocer's/vegetable store**	. . . die Gemüsehandlung *dee germewserhandloong*
. . . **grocer's**	. . . das Lebensmittelgeschäft *das laibensmittelgersheft*
. . . **jeweller's**	. . . der Juwelier *dair yooveleer*
. . . **launderette**	. . . der Waschsalon *dair vash-zalon*
. . . **newsagent's**	. . . der Zeitungshändler *dair tsytoongz-hendler*
. . . **optician**	. . . der Optiker *dair optiker*
. . . **post office**	. . . das Postamt *das posstamt*
. . . **shoe-repairer's**	. . . der Schuhmacher *dair shoomakher*
. . . **supermarket**	. . . der Supermarkt *dair zoopermarkt*
. . . **toy shop**	. . . das Spielwarengeschäft *das shpeelvaaren-gersheft*

At a department store

Department Store	das Kaufhaus *das kowfhows*
Where are the . . . ?	Wo sind die . . . ? *voh zint dee . . . ?*
. . . records	. . . Schallplatten *shalplatten*
. . . sports goods	. . . Sportartikel *shportartikel*
. . . books	. . . Bücher *bewkher*
Which floor is it on?	Im welchem Stock? *im velkhem shtok?*
On the ground floor	Im Erdgeschoß *im airdgershoss*
In the basement	Im Untergeschoß *im oontergershoss*
On the first/second floor	Im ersten/zweiten Stock *im airsten/tsvyten shtok*
Camping Equipment	Campingzubehör *kemping-tsooberhur*
Toiletries	Toilettenartikel *twaletten-artikel*
Clothing and Shoes	Kleider und Schuhe *klyder oont shooer*
Electrical Goods	Elektrowaren *elektrovaaren*
Food	Lebensmittel *laibenzmittel*
Optical Goods	Optiker *optiker*
Photographic Equipment	Fotoartikel *fohto-artikel*
Repairs	Reparaturen *reparatooren*

Clothes and shoes

- For size conversions, see page 131.

I'd like something . . .	Ich möchte etwas . . . *ikh murkhter etvas . . .*
. . . for me/her/him	. . . für mich/sie/ihn *fewr mikh/zee/een*
. . . to match this	. . . was dazu paßt *vas datsoo passt*
I take size . . .	Ich habe Größe . . . *ikh haaber grurser . . .*
(Where) can I try it on?	(Wo) kann ich es anprobieren? *(voh) kan ikh es anprobeeren?*
Is there a mirror?	Gibt es einen Spiegel? *gipt es I-nen shpeegel?*
It doesn't fit	Es sitzt nicht sehr gut *es zitst nikht zair goot*

It's too . . .	Es ist zu . . . *es ist tsoo . . .*
. . . long/short	. . . lang/kurz *lang/koorts*
. . . tight/loose	. . . eng/weit *eng/vyt*
. . . big/small	. . . groß/klein *grohs/klyn*

Can you alter it?	Können sie es ändern? *kurnen zee es endern?*
I don't like the style/colour	Der Stil/die Farbe gefällt mir nicht *dair shteel/dee faarber gerfelt meer nikht*

Do you have this in green?	Haben Sie das in grün? *haaben zee das in grewn?*
Does it have to be handwashed?	Muß man das mit der Hand waschen? *moos man das mit dair hant vashen?*

You may hear:

Welche Größe haben Sie? *velkher grurser haaben zee?*	What size do you take?
Wir haben es nicht in dieser Farbe/Ihrer Größe *veer haaben es nikht in deezer faarber/eerer grurser*	We don't have it in that colour/your size
Der Spiegel/die Umkleidekabine ist da drüben *dair shpeegel/dee oomlyder-kabeener ist da drewben*	The mirror/fitting room is over there

Colours and Fabrics

black	schwarz *shvarts*	blue	blau *bl-ow*
brown	braun *brown*	green	grün *grewn*
orange	orange *oronzh*	yellow	gelb *gelp*
red	rot *roht.*	white	weiß *vys*
light (grey)	hell (grau) *hell (gr-ow)*	dark (pink)	dunkel (rosa) *doonkel (rohza)*
cotton	Baumwolle *bowmvoller*	wool	Wolle *voller*
leather	Leder *laider*	silk	Seide *zyder*
suede	Wildleder *viltlaider*	synthetic	Synthetisch *zewntaitish*

Clothes

belt	der Gürtel
	dair gewrtel
blouse	die Bluse
	dee bloozer
bra	der Büstenhalter
	dair bewstenhalter
coat	der Mantel
	dair mantel
dress	das Kleid
	das klyt
handbag	die Handtasche
	dee hant-tasher
hat	der Hut
	dair hoot
jacket	die Jacke
	dee yakker
jersey	der Pullover
	dair pool-over
pyjamas	der Schlafanzug
	dair shlaaf-antsoog
raincoat	der Regenmantel
	dair raigenmantel
shirt	das Hemd
	das hemt
shorts	Shorts
	'shorts'
skirt	der Rock
	dair rok
socks	Socken
	zokken
stockings	Strümpfe
	shtrewmpfer
swimsuit	der Badeanzug
	dair baaderantsoog

tie	die Krawatte
	dee kravatter
tights	Strumpfhose
	shtroompf-hohzer
trousers	die Hose
	dee hohzer
(under)pants	die Unterhose
	dee oonterhohzer

Shoes

I'd like a pair of . . .	Ich möchte ein Paar . . .
	ikh murkhter I-n paar . . .
. . . boots	. . . Stiefel
	shteefel
. . . trainers	. . . Turnschuhe
	toorn-shooer
. . . walking boots	. . . Wanderschuhe
	vander-shooer
Do you have a larger/smaller pair?	Haben Sie ein größeres/ kleineres Paar?
	haaben zee I-n grurseres/ klyneres paar?
Do you have any . . . ?	Haben Sie . . . ?
	haaben zee . . . ?
. . . insoles	. . . Einlegesohlen
	I-nlaiger-zohlen
. . . laces	. . . Schnürsenkel
	shnewrzenkel
. . . polish	. . . Schuhcreme
	shookraimer
Can I try them on?	Kann ich sie anprobieren?
	kan ikh zee anprobeeren?
They're a bit uncomfortable	Sie sind ein bißchen unbequem
	zee zint I-n bisskhen oon-ber-kvaim

At the hairdresser's/barber's

- Hairdresser's in Germany are usually closed on Mondays.

Can you recommend a hairdresser?	Können Sie einen Friseur empfehlen? *kurnen zee I-nen frizur empfailen?*
I'd like an appointment for . . .	Ich möchte einen Termin am . . . *ikh murkhter I-nen tairmeen am . . .*
Just a trim, please	Nur etwas nachschneiden, bitte *noor etvas nakhshnyden bitter*
A cut and blow-dry	Waschen und fönen, bitte *vashen oont furnen bitter*
Not too short/long	Nicht zu kurz/lang *nikht tsoo koorts/lang*
A bit more off here	Hier etwas kürzer, bitte *heer etvas kewrtser bitter*
Would you trim my beard/ moustache	Können Sie mir bitte den Bart/den Schnurrbart stutzen? *kurnen zee meer bitter dain bart/dain shnoorbart shtootsen?*
I'd like . . .	Ich möchte . . . *ikh murkhter . . .*
. . . the same style again	. . . nochmal den gleichen Schnitt *nokhmal dain glykhen shnit*
. . . highlights	. . . Strähnchen *shtrainkhen*
. . . conditioner	. . . eine Haarschnellkur *I-ner haarshnelkoor*

Photographic

I'd like a film/two films for this camera	Ich möchte einen Film/zwei Filme für diesen Photoapparat *ikh murkhter I-nen film/tsvy filmer fewr deezen fohto-aparaat*
black and white film	Schwarzweißfilm *shvaarts-vys-film*
colour film	Farbnegativfilm *faarbnegateef-film*
colour slide film	Farbdiafilm *farb-deeafilm*
24/36 exposures	24/36 Aufnahmen *feer-oont-tsvantsig/sekhs-oont-drysig owfnaamen*
I'd like some passport photos taken	Ich möchte Paßbilder machen lassen *ikh murkhter pasbilder makhen lassen*
Is processing included?	Ist der Preis mit Entwicklung? *ist dair prys mit entvikloong?*
How much is processing?	Was kostet die Entwicklung? *vas kostet dee entvikloong?*
How long will it take?	Wie lange dauert es? *vee langer dowert es?*
I'd like . . . copies/ enlargements	Ich möchte . . . Abzüge/ Vergrößerungen *ikh murkhter . . . aptsewger/ fairgrurseroongen*
Can you repair my camera?	Können Sie meinen Photoapparat reparieren? *kurnen zee mynen fohto-aparaat repareeren?*
Do you have any batteries?	Haben Sie Batterien? *haaben zee bateree-en?*

At the chemist's

- There are two types of chemist's in Germany:
  - The *Apotheke* is a pharmacist's. It can make up prescriptions and sell drugs but it does not sell toiletries, films etc. When closed, the address of the nearest chemist's which is open is displayed in the window. At night, ring the doorbell for service.
  - The *Drogerie* sells toiletries, non-prescription drugs etc. **NB** *Gift* means 'poison'.

Where's the nearest (all-night) chemist's?	Wo ist die nächste Apotheke (mit Nachtdienst)? *voh ist dee nekhster apotaiker (mit nakhtdeenst)?*
I want something for ...	Ich möchte etwas gegen ... *ikh murkhter etvas gaigen ...*
... diarrhoea	... Durchfall *doorkhfal*
... a headache	... Kopfschmerzen *kopfshmairtsen*
... insect-bites	... Insektenstiche *inzektenshtikher*
... a sore throat	... Halsschmerzen *hals-shmairtsen*
... sunburn	... Sonnenbrand *zonnenbrant*
... an upset stomach	... Magenverstimmung *maagen-fairshtimoong*
Can I get it without prescription?	Brauche ich ein Rezept dafür? *browkher ikh I-n retsept dafewr?*
It's for an adult/a child	Es ist für einen Erwachsenen/ein Kind *es ist fewr I-nen airvakhsenen/I-n kint*

Groceries

- For weights and measures conversions, see page 129.
- For items of food and drink, see page 155.

Can I help myself?	Kann ich mich selbst bedienen? *kan ikh mikh zelbst berdeenen?*
May I have a plastic bag?	Kann ich eine Plastiktüte haben? *kan ikh I-ner plastik-tewter haaben?*
one/some of those	eins/einige von denen *I-ns/I-niger fon dainen*
a piece/two pieces of . . .	ein Stück/zwei Stück . . . *I-n shtewk/tsvy shtewk . . .*
a slice/two slices of . . .	eine Scheibe/zwei Scheiben . . . *I-ner shyber/tsvy shyben . . .*
a bottle of . . .	eine Flasche . . . *I-ner flasher . . .*
a can/tin of . . .	eine Dose . . . *I-ner dohzer . . .*
a jar of . . .	ein Glas . . . *yn glaas . . .*
a packet of . . .	eine Packung/eine Tüte . . . *I-ner pakkoong/I-ner tewter . . .*
a kilo of . . .	ein Kilo . . . *I-n keelo . . .*
half a kilo of . . .	ein halbes Kilo . . . *I-n halbes keelo . . .*
a pound of . . .	ein Pfund . . . *I-n pfoont . . .*
200 grammes of . . .	200 Gramm . . . *tsvy hoondert gram . . .*
a litre of . . .	ein Liter . . . *I-n leeter . . .*

Miscellaneous

I'm looking for a present for . . .	Ich suche ein Geschenk für . . . *ikh sookher I-n gershenk fewr . . .*
Do you have anything in gold/silver?	Haben Sie etwas in Gold/Silber? *haaben zee etvas in golt/zilber?*
Is this real silver?	Ist das Echtsilber? *ist das ekht-zilber*
I want a small present	Ich möchte ein kleines Geschenk *ikh murkhter I-n klyn-es gershenk*
I'd like a toy/game	Ich möchte ein Spielzeug/Spiel *ikh murkhter I-n shpeel-tsoyg/shpeel*
Do you have any records by . . . ?	Haben Sie Schallplatten von . . . ? *haaben zee shaal-platten fon . . . ?*
I'd like a souvenir	Ich möchte ein Andenken *ikh murkhter I-n andenken*

It's for . . .	Es ist für . . . *es ist fewr . . .*
. . . my girlfriend/boyfriend	. . . meine Freundin/meinen Freund *myner froyndin/mynen froynt*
. . . my wife/husband	. . . meine Frau/meinen Mann *myner frow/mynen man*
. . . my parents	. . . meine Eltern *myner eltern*

- Credit cards are not yet widely used for payment in shops or restaurants, but they are accepted in most hotels. It is useful to acquire a Eurocheque card and book before your departure.
- Traveller's cheques are an accepted means of payment, though you will not get such a good exchange rate as in a bank.
- Banking hours: 8.30–13.00 and 14.30–16.00 (17.30 on Thursdays). Outside these hours, look for currency-exchange shops (*Geldwechsel*, or *Wechselstube*).

  Germany: 1DM (*Deutsche Mark*, or just *Mark*) = 100Pf (*Pfennig*)

  Austria: 1S (*Schilling*) = 100g (*Groschen*)

  Switzerland: 1Fr (*Franken*) = 100Rp (*Rappen*)

Bank

Where is the nearest bank?	Wo ist die nächste Bank/ Sparkasse? *voh ist dee nekhster bank/ shpaarkasser?*
I'd like to change some dollars/pounds into Marks	Ich möchte Dollar/Pfund in D-Mark wechseln *ikh murkhter dollar/pfoont in dai-maark vekhseln*
I'd like to cash a traveller's cheque/Eurocheque	Ich möchte einen Reisescheck/Euroscheck einlösen *ikh murkhter I-nen ryzreshek/ oyroshek I-nlurzen*
I'd like to buy some Marks with my credit card	Ich möchte D-Mark mit meiner Kreditkarte kaufen *ikh murkhter dai-maark mit myner kredeetkaarter kowfen*
What's the exchange rate?	Wie ist der Kurs? *vee ist dair koorz?*
I'm expecting money from England	Ich erwarte Geld aus England *ikh ervaarter gelt ows englant*
Has it arrived?	Ist es schon da? *ist es shohn daa?*
Here is my passport	Hier ist mein Paß *heer ist myn pass*
I'd like notes/some small change	Ich möchte Scheine/etwas Kleingeld *ikh murkhter shyner/etvas klyngelt*
Where should I sign?	Wo muß ich unterschreiben? *voh moos ikh oonter-shryben?*
I'd like to deposit this money	Ich möchte dieses Geld einzahlen *ikh murkhter deezes gelt I-ntsaalen*

Services

I'd like to transfer some money	Ich möchte Geld überweisen *ikh murkhter gelt ewbervyzen*
I'd like to withdraw some money	Ich möchte Geld abheben *ikh murkhter gelt abhaiben*

You may hear:

Wieviel möchten Sie wechseln? *veefeel murkhtern zee vekhseln?*	How much would you like to change?
Kann ich Ihren Paß haben? *kan ikh eeren pass haaben?*	May I see your passport?
Ohne Paß können wir Reiseschecks nicht einlösen *ohner pass kurnen veer ryzersheks nicht I-nlurzen*	We can't change traveller's cheques without a passport
Bitte füllen Sie dieses Formular aus *bitter fewlen zee deezes formoolaar ows*	Please fill in this form
Bitte unterschreiben Sie hier *bitter oontershryben zee heer*	Please sign here
Nehmen Sie dieses Papier/ diese Nummer *naimen zee deezes papeer/ deezer noomer*	Take this piece of paper/ number
Gehen Sie an Kasse Nummer ... *gaien zee an kasser noomer*	Go to counter number ...
Wie soll ich Ihnen das Geld geben? *vee zoll ikh eenen das gelt gaiben*	How would you like the money
Das ist Ihre Quittung *das ist eerer kvittoong*	Here's your receipt

I'd like to open an account

Ich möchte ein Konto
eröffnen
ikh murkhter I-n konto air-urfnen

Where should I sign?

Wo muß ich unterschreiben?
voh moos ikh oonter-shryben?

I want to pay this into my account

Ich möchte das auf mein
Konto einzahlen
ikh murkhter das owf myn konto I-n-tsaalen

You may see:

Bank	Bank
Devisen	Foreign currency
Geldautomat	Cash dispenser
Geldwechsel	Currency exchange
Kasse	Cashier
Schalterstunden **Schalterzeiten**	Opening hours
Sorten	Foreign currency
Sparkasse	Savings bank
Wechselstube	Currency exchange

NB '*Spielbank*' is a casino.

You may hear:

Das macht ...
das makht

That comes to ...

**Bitte füllen sie dieses
Zollformular aus**
*bitter fewlen zee deezes
tsollformoolaar ows*

Please fill in this customs
declaration

Unterschreiben Sie hier
oontershryben zee heer

Sign here

Gehen Sie an Schalter (4)
gai-en zee an shallter (feer)

Go to counter (4)

Post office

Opening times

Germany
8.00–18.00; Saturday 8.00–13.00

Austria
8.00–12.00, 14.00–17.00; Saturday 8.00–10/12.00

Switzerland
7.30–12.00, 13.30–18.30; Saturday 8.00–11.00

Where is the nearest post office/letterbox?	Wo ist das nächste Postamt/ Briefkasten? *voh ist das nekhster posstamt breefkasten?*
An 80-pfennig stamp, please	Eine Briefmarke zu 80 Pfennig, bitte *I-ner breefmarker tsoo akhtsig pfennig, bitter*
5 1-mark stamps, please	Fünf Briefmarken zu 1 Mark, bitte *fewnf breefmaarken tsoo I-ner maark bitter*
What's the cost of . . . ?	Was kostet . . . ? *vas kostet . . . ?*
. . . a letter to America	. . . ein Brief nach Amerika *I-n breef nakh amerika*
. . . a post-card to England	. . . eine Postkarte nach England *I-ner postkaarter nakh englant*
. . . this parcel	. . . dieses Paket *deezes pakait*
Can you weight this letter/ this parcel?	Können Sie bitte diesen Brief/ dieses Paket wiegen? *kurnen zee bitter deezen breef/deezes pakait veegen?*

I'd like to send it . . .	Ich möchte es . . . schicken *ikh murkhter es . . . shiken*
. . . by air mail	. . . per Luftpost *pair looftposst*
. . . express delivery	. . . per Eilpost *pair I-lposst*
. . . letter post	. . . als Brief *als breef*
. . . parcel post	. . . als Paket *als pakait*
. . . surface mail	. . . per Normaltarif *pair normaaltareef*
. . . registered delivery	. . . per Einschreiben *pair I-nshryben*
I'd like to cash an international money order	Ich möchte eine internationale Postanweisung einlösen *ikh murkhter I-ner internatsionaaler posstanvyzoong I-nlurzen*
Is there any post for me?	Ist Post für mich da? *ist posst fewr mikh daa?*

You may see:

Ausland	Foreign (counter)
Briefkasten	Letter box
Briefmarkenautomat	Stamp dispenser
Fernsprecher	Telephone
Nächste Leerung	Next collection
Pakete	Parcels
Postlagernde Sendungen	Post restante
Postwertzeichen	Stamps
Sondermarken	Commemorative stamps

Telephone

- Most telephone boxes have instructions in English and diagrams as well as German. International calls can also be made from most of them, or you can go to the counter marked *Ferngespräche* in larger post offices, where you will be allocated a telephone booth. You pay after you have finished your call.
- When making phone-calls abroad, remember to omit the first 0 of the town code following the country code: eg when phoning Cambridge from Germany, dial 0044 (England), then 223 (not 0223), followed by the number.
- On the phone, 2 is pronounced *tsvoh*, to avoid confusion with 3 (*dry*).

Where's ... ?	Wo ist ... ? *voh ist ... ?*
... the telephone	... das Telefon *... das telefohn*
... the nearest telephone box	... die nächste Telefonzelle *dee nekhster telefohntseller*
May I use the phone?	Darf ich das Telefon benutzen? *daarf ikh das telefohn bernootsen?*
Hallo, this is ...	Hallo, hier ... *hallo, heer ...*
May I speak to ...	Kann ich ... sprechen, bitte? *kan ikh ... shprekhen bitter?*
May I have extension number ... ?	Ich möchte Apparat ... *ikh murkhter aparaat ...*
I'll phone again later	Ich rufe wieder an *ikh roofer veeder an*
When can I get him/her?	Wann kann ich ihn/sie erreichen? *van kan ikh een/zee errykhen?*

Can I leave a message?	Können Sie etwas ausrichten?
	kurnen zee etvas owsrikhten?
My name is . . .	Ich heiße . . .
	ikh hysser . . .
Please tell him/her I called	Bitte sagen Sie ihm/ihr, daß ich angerufen habe
	bitter zaagen zee eem/eer, das ikh angeroofen haaber
Could you ask him/her to phone me?	Können Sie ihn/sie bitten, mich anzurufen?
	kurnen zee een/zee bitten, mikh antsooroofern?
between 5 and 7 o'clock	zwischen 5 und 7 Uhr
	tsvishen fewnf oont zeeben oor
My phone number is	Meine Telefonnummer ist . . .
	myner telefohnnoomer ist

Operator

What's the code for . . . ?	Was ist die Vorwahl für . . . ?
	vas ist dee fohrvaal fewr . . . ?
I'd like to make a call to America	Ich möchte nach Amerika anrufen
	ikh murkhter nakh amerika anroofen
I need the telephone directory for . . .	Ich brauche das Telefonbuch für . . .
	ikh browkher das telefohnbookh fewr . . .
What's the number for (international) directory enquiries?	Welche Nummer hat die (internationale) Auskunft?
	velkher noomer hat dee (internatsionaaler) owskoonft?
What's the number for the (international) operator?	Welche Nummer hat die (internationale) Vermittlung?
	velkher noomer hat dee (internatsionaaler) fairmitloong?

Could you help me to get this number?	Können Sie mir helfen, diese Nummer zu bekommen? *kurnen zee meer helfen, deezer noomer tsoo berkommen?*
I can't get through	Ich komme nicht durch *ikh kommer nikht doorkh*
I want to make a reverse charge call	Ich möchte ein R-gespräch *ikh murkhter I-n air-gershprekh*
I've been cut off	Ich bin unterbrochen worden *ikh bin oonterbrokhen vorden*
I dialled the wrong number	Ich habe mich verwählt *ikh haaber mikh fairvailt*
I was given the wrong number	Man hat mich falsch verbunden *man hat mikh falsh fairboonden*
What did the call cost?	Was hat das Gespräch gekostet? *vas hat das gershpraikh gerkostet?*

You may see:

Auskunft	Enquiries
Auslandsgespräche	Foreign calls
Bitte zahlen	Please insert more money
Inlandsgespräche	Phone calls within the country
Münzfreier Notruf	Free calls to emergency services
Münzeinwurf	Insert coins
Münzrückgabe	Returned coins

You may hear:

Wer ist am Apparat? *vair ist am aparaat?*	Who's speaking?
Einen Moment, bitte *I-nen moment bitter*	Just a minute; hold on, please
Bleiben Sie am Apparat *blyben zee am aparaat*	Hold the line
Er/sie ist zur Zeit nicht da *er/zee ist tsoor tsyt nikht daa*	He/she isn't in at the moment
Es ist besetzt *es ist berzetst*	The line's engaged
Es antwortet niemand *es antvortet neemant*	There's no answer
Können Sie später wieder anrufen? *kurnen zee shpaiter veeder anroofen?*	Could you phone back later?
Kann er/sie Sie zurückrufen? *kan er/zee zee tsoorewkroofen?*	Can he/she phone you back?
Kann ich ihm/ihr etwas ausrichten? *kan ikh eem/eer etvas owsrikhten?*	Can I give him/her a message?
Sind Sie telefonisch zu erreichen? *zint zee telefohnish tsoo errykhen?*	Can you be reached by phone?
Sie haben sich verwählt *zee haaben zikh fairvailt*	You've got the wrong number
Welche Nummer haben Sie gewählt? *velkher noomer haaben zee gervailt?*	What number did you dial?

Repairs

Can you repair this?	Können Sie das reparieren? *kurnen zee das repareeren?*
There's something wrong with this	Etwas stimmt nicht damit *etvas shtimt nikht daamit*
It works sometimes	Es funktioniert manchmal *es foonktsioneert mankhmaal*
It doesn't work	Es funktioniert nicht *es fooktsioneert nikht*
It's jammed	Es klemmt *es klemt*
It's broken	Es ist kaputt *es ist kapoot*
I can't close/open it	Ich kann es nicht zumachen/aufmachen *ikh kan es nikht tsoomakhen/owfmakhen*
How much will it cost?	Wieviel kostet es? *veefeel kostet es?*
How long will it take?	Wie lange dauert es? *vee langer dowert es?*
I'm here for 2 more days/weeks	Ich bin noch 2 Tagen/Wochen hier *ikh bin nokh tsvy taager/vokhen heer*
Is it worth it?	Lohnt es sich? *lohnt es sikh?*

You may hear:

Es lohnt sich nicht *es lohnt sikh nikht*	It's not worth it
Das läßt sich nicht reparieren *das lesst sikh nikht repareeren*	It can't be repaired

Dieses Modell wird nicht mehr hergestellt *deezes model virt nikht mair hairgershtelt*	This model isn't produced any more
Wir müssen die Ersatzteile bestellen *veer mewssen dee airzatstyler bershtellen*	We'll have to order the parts
Es ist in 2 Tagen/Wochen fertig *es ist in tsvy taagen/vokhen fairtig*	It'll be ready in 2 days/weeks
Wir müssen es wegschicken *veer mewssen es vaig-shiken*	We'll have to send it away
Am besten lassen Sie es zu Hause reparieren *am besten lassen zee es tsoo howzer repareeren*	It would be better to have it repaired at home

Shoes

Where can I get my shoes mended?	Wo kann ich diese Schuhe reparieren lassen? *voh kan ikh deezer shoo-er repareeren lassen?*
Can you repair these shoes?	Können Sie diese Schuhe reparieren? *kurnen zee deezer shoo-er repareeren?*
Can you stitch this?	Können Sie das nähen? *kurnen zee das nai-en?*
I want new soles/heels	Ich möchte neue Sohlen/Absätze *ikh murkhter noyer sohlen/apsetser*
When will they be ready?	Wann sind sie fertig? *van zint zee fairtig?*

Lost property

- Look for the sign *Fundamt*, *Fundbüro* or *Fundsachen*. In smaller towns, this is often at the town hall. In case of thefts, go to the police station.

Where is . . . ?	Wo ist . . . ? *voh ist . . . ?*
. . . the lost property office	. . . das Fundbüro *das foontbewroh*
. . . the police station	. . . das Polizeirevier *das polits-I-reveer*
I'd like to report . . .	Ich möchte . . . melden *ikh murkhter . . . melden*
. . . a loss	. . . einen Verlust . . . *I-nen fairloost*
. . . a theft	. . . einen Diebstahl . . . *I-nen deepshtaal*
My . . . has been stolen	Mein/meine . . . ist gestohlen worden *myn/myner . . . ist gerstohlen vorden*

I've lost a/an/some . . .	Ich habe . . . verloren *ikh haaber . . . fairlohren*
. . . backpack	. . . einen Rucksack . . . *I-nen rookzak*
. . . camera	. . . einen Fotoapparat . . . *I-nen fohto-aparaat*
. . . cheque book	. . . eine Scheckheft . . . *I-n shek-heft*
. . . cheque card	. . . eine Scheckkarte . . . *I-ner shek-kaarter*
. . . credit card	. . . eine Kreditkarte . . . *I-ner kredeetkaarter*
. . . keys	. . . Schlüssel . . . *shlewsel*

... **money**	... Geld ... *gelt*
... **purse**	... ein Portemonnaie ... *I-n portmonai*
... **radio**	... ein Radio ... *I-n radioh*
... **suitcase**	... einen Koffer ... *I-nen koffer*
... **ticket**	... eine Fahrkarte ... *I-ner faarkaarter*
... **traveller's cheques**	... Reiseschecks ... *ryzersheks*
... **umbrella**	... einen Regenschirm ... *I-nen raigensheerm*
... **wallet**	... eine Brieftasche ... *I-ner breeftasher*

It's made of ...	Es ist aus ... *es ist ows ...*
... **cloth**	... Stoff *shtoff*
... **cotton**	... Baumwolle *bowmvoller*
... **gold**	... Gold *golt*
... **leather**	... Leder *laider*
... **plastic**	... Plaṣtik *plastik*
... **metal**	... Metall *metal*
... **silver**	... Silber *zilber*

126   ● For colours and fabrics, see page 105.

It's worth about . . .	Es ist gegen . . . wert *es ist gaigen . . . vairt*
It's red with a blue stripe	Es ist rot mit einem blauen Streifen *es ist roht mit I-nem blowen shtry-fen*
It has my name . . .	Es hat meinen Namen . . . *es hat mynen naamen . . .*
. . . on it	. . . darauf *daarowf*
. . . in one corner	. . . in einer Ecke *in I-ner ekker*
. . . inside	. . . darin *daarin*
I lost it at the station	Ich habe es auf dem Bahnhof verloren *ikh haaber es owf daim baanhohf fairloren*
I lost it . . .	Ich habe es . . . verloren *ikh haaber es . . . fairloren*
. . . at about 3 o'clock	. . . gegen 3 Uhr *gaigen dry oor*
. . . today	. . . heute *hoyter*
. . . yesterday	. . . gestern *gestern*
I don't know when/where I lost it	Ich weiß nicht, wo/wann ich es verloren habe *ikh vys nikht voh/van ikh es fairloren haaber*

● For times, see page 135.

My name is . . .	Mein Name ist . . . *myn naamer ist*
My address is . . .	Meine Adresse ist . . . *myner adresser ist*

127

Churches and religious services

- It is usually possible to go into most churches, cathedrals etc except when a service is in progress.
- In many towns you will find some services are conducted in English. Ask at the local tourist office for details.
- Photography is not always permitted – ask before using your camera. It is usually possible to buy postcards instead.

Where is . . . ?	Wo ist . . . ? *voh ist . . . ?*
. . . the Catholic church	. . . die katholische Kirche *dee katohlisher keerkher*
. . . the Protestant church	. . . die evangelische Kirche *dee evangailisher keerkher*
. . . the synagogue	. . . die Synagoge *dee zewnagohger*
At what time is . . . ?	Wann beginnt . . . ? *van bergint . . . ?*
. . . family service	. . . der Familiengottesdienst *dair fameeliengottesdeenst*
. . . the mass	. . . die Messe *dee messer*
. . . the service	. . . der Gottesdienst *dair gottesdeenst*
Is there a . . . who speaks English?	Gibt es einen . . . , der Englisch spricht? *gipt es I-nen . . . , dair english shprikht?*
. . . minister . . .	. . . Pfarrer . . . *pfarrer*
. . . priest . . .	. . . Priester . . . *preester*
. . . rabbi . . .	. . . Rabbiner . . . *rabeener*

ESSENTIAL INFORMATION

Conversion tables

Fluids

1 imperial gallon = 4.55 litres   1 US gallon = 3.8 litres
1 litre = 1.76 imp. pints   1 litre = 2.08 US pints

litres	5	10	15	20	25	30	35	40	45	50
imp. gal	1.1	2.2	3.3	4.4	5.5	6.6	7.7	8.8	9.9	11.0
US gal	1.3	2.6	3.9	5.2	6.5	7.8	9.1	10.4	11.7	13.0

Kilometres to miles

1 km = 0.62 miles

km	5	10	20	30	40	50	60	70	80	90	100	150	200
miles	3	6	12	19	25	31	37	44	50	56	.62	93	124

Miles to kilometres

1 mile = 1.609 km

miles	5	10	20	30	40	50	60	70	80	90	100	150	200
km	8	16	32	48	64	80	97	113	129	145	161	241	322

Weights

1 kilo = 1 000 grams = 2.2 lbs   1 lb = 454 grams
500 g = 1.1 lbs   ½ lb = 227 grams
200 g = 7 ozs   1 oz = 28 grams
100 g = 3.5 ozs

Length

centimetres to inches: multiply by 0.39
inches to centimetres: multiply by 2.54

metric	imperial		imperial	metric
1 mm	0.039	in	1 in	25.4 mm/2.54 cm
1 cm	0.39	in	1ft	30.48 cm/0.305 m
1 m	39.40	in	1 yd	91.44 cm/0.914 m
	3.28	ft		
	1.09	yds		

Notices

Ausfahrt	Exit (vehicles)
Ausgang	Exit
Auskunft	Information
Außer Betrieb	Out of order
Belegt	No vacancies
Besetzt	Occupied
Bitte nicht stören	Do not disturb
Damen	Ladies
Drücken	Push
Einfahrt	Entrance (vehicles)
Eingang	Entrance
Eintritt frei	Entrance free
Gefahr	Danger
Geschlossen	Closed
Heiß	Hot
Herren	Men
Kalt	Cold
Kasse	Till/cash desk
Kein Zutritt	No entrance
Nicht berühren	Do not touch
Notausgang	Emergency exit
Notruf	Emergency phone
Rauchen verboten	No smoking
Selbstbedienung	Self-service
Stammtisch	Reserved for regular customers
Ziehen	Pull
Zimmer frei	Vacancies
Zu verkaufen	For sale
Zu vermieten	For hire/rent

Clothing sizes

Waist/Chest measurements

Inches	28	30	32	34	36	38	40	42	44	46
cms	71	76	80	87	91	97	102	107	112	117

Women

Dresses

European	36	38	40	42	44	46
British	10	12	14	16	18	20
American	8	10	12	14	16	18

Shoes

European	36	37	38	39	40	41
British	4	4½	5½	6	6½	7½
American	5½	6	7	7½	8	9

Men

Jackets/Coats

European	46	48	50	52	54	56
British/US	36	38	40	42	44	46

Shirts

European	36	37	38	39	41	42	43
British/US	14	14½	15	15½	16	16½	17

Shoes

European	38	39	41	42	43	44	45
British/US	5	6	7	8	8½/9	9½/10	11

Numbers

0	null	*nul*	11	elf	*elf*
1	eins	*I-ns*	12	zwölf	*tsvurlf*
2	zwei	*tsvy*	13	dreizehn	*drytsain*
3	drei	*dry*	14	vierzehn	*feertsain*
4	vier	*feer*	15	fünfzehn	*fewnftsain*
5	fünf	*fewnf*	16	sechzehn	*zekhtsain*
6	sechs	*zekhs*	17	siebzehn	*zeeptsain*
7	sieben	*zeeben*	18	achtzehn	*akhtsain*
8	acht	*akht*	19	neunzehn	*noyntsain*
9	neun	*noyn*	20	zwanzig	*tsvantsig*
10	zehn	*tsain*			

21 einundzwanzig   *I-n-oont-tsvantsig*

ie 'one-and-twenty'. All 'tens and units' numbers work like this.

30	**dreißig**	*drysig*
40	**vierzig**	*feertsig*
50	**fünfzig**	*fewnftsig*
60	**sechzig**	*zekhtsig*
70	**siebzig**	*zeeptsig*
80	**achtzig**	*akhtsig*
90	**neunzig**	*noyntsig*
100	**hundert**	*hoondert*
101	**hunderteins**	*hoondert-yns*
200	**zweihundert**	*tsvy-hoondert*
1 000	**(ein)tausend**	*(I-n) towzent*
1 100	**tausendeinhundert**	*towzent-I-yn-hoondert*
2 000	**zweitausend**	*tsvy-towzent*
1 000 000	**eine Million**	*I-ner miliohn*

4.5%   4.5 Prozent
feer komma fewnf prohtsent

$3 + 2 = 5$ drei plus zwei ist gleich fünf
dry ploos tsvy ist glykh fewnf

$3 - 2 = 1$ drei minus zwei ist gleich eins
dry minoos tsvy ist glykh I-ns

$3 \times 2 = 6$ drei mal zwei ist gleich sechs
dry maal tsvy ist glykh zekhs

1st	erste *airster*	once	einmal *I-nmaal*
2nd	zweite *tsvyter*	twice	zweimal *tsvymaal*
3rd	dritte *dritter*	six times	sechsmal *zekhsmaal*
4th	vierte *feerter*		
10th	zehnte *tsainter*		
20th	zwanzigste *tsvantsigster*		

Months

January	Januar *yanooaar*	**July**	Juli *yooli*
February	Februar *febroɔaar*	**August**	August *owgoost*
March	März *mairts*	**September**	September *zeptember*
April	April *apreel*	**October**	Oktober *oktohber*
May	Mai *my*	**November**	November *nohvember*
June	Juni *yooni*	**December**	Dezember *daitsember*

Days

Sunday	Sonntag *zontaag*	**Thursday**	Donnerstag *donnerztaag*
Monday	Montag *mohntaag*	**Friday**	Freitag *frytaag*
Tuesday	Dienstag *deenstaag*	**Saturday**	Samstaag *zamztaag* Sonnabend (N. Germany) *zonaabent*
Wednesday	Mittwoch *mitvokh*		

Seasons and dates

Spring	Frühling *frewling*
Summer	Sommer *zommer*
Autumn	Herbst *hairpst*
Winter	Winter *vinter*

in (the) summer	im Sommer *im zommer*
What's the date today?	Der wievielte ist heute? *dair veefeelter ist hoyter?*
It's the 3rd August	Es ist der dritte August *es ist dair dritter owgoost*
(at the) beginning/end of June	Anfang/Ende Juni *anfang/ender yooni*
(in the) middle of May	Mitte Mai *mitter my*
by July	bis Juli *bis yooli*
in October	im Oktober *im oktohber*
since August	seit August *zyt owgoost*
until September	bis September *bis zeptember*
last/next month	letzten/nächsten Monat *letsten/nekhsten mohnaat*
a month ago	vor einem Monat *for I-nem mohnaat*
on Tuesday	am Dienstag *am deenstaag*
last/next Friday	letzten/nächsten Freitag *letsten/nekhsten frytaag*
on Thursdays	Donnerstags *donnerztagz*
on 19th July	am neunzehnten Juli *am noyntsainten yooli*
today	heute *hoyter*
tomorrow	morgen *morgen*

yesterday	gestern
	gestern
two days ago	vor zwei Tagen
	for tsvy taagen
in four days' time	in vier Tagen
	in feer taagen
at the weekend	am Wochenende
	am vokhenender

Time

What time is it?	Wieviel Uhr ist es?
	veefeel oor ist es?
It's . . .	Es ist . . .
	est ist . . .
. . . 1.00	. . . ein Uhr
	I-n oor
. . . 1.05	. . . fünf nach eins
	fewnf nakh I-ns
. . . 1.15	. . . Viertel nach eins
	feertel nakh I-ns
. . . 1.20	. . . zwanzig nach eins
	tsvantsig nakh I-ns
. . . 1.30	. . . halb zwei
	halp tsvy
. . . 1.40	. . . zwanzig vor zwei
	tsvantsig for tsvy
. . . 1.45	. . . Viertel vor zwei
	feertel for tsvy
. . . 1.50	. . . zehn vor zwei
	tsain for tsvy
. . . 12.00 midday	. . . zwölf Uhr Mittag
midnight	Mitternacht
	tsvurlf oor mittaag
	mitternakht
in the morning	morgens
	morgerns

135

in the afternoon	nachmittags *nakhmitaagz*
in the evening	abends *aabents*

Public holidays

National holidays are shown: there are local variations.

Austria = **A**   Germany = **D**   Switzerland = **CH**

1 Jan	New Year's Day *Neujahr*	A	D	CH
6 Jan	Epiphany *Dreikönigstag*	A		
1 May	Labour Day *Tag der Arbeit*	A	D	
17 June	German Unity Day *Tag der Deutschen Einheit*		D	
1 Aug	National Day *Nationalfeiertag*			CH
15 Aug	Assumption *Mariä Himmelfahrt*	A		
26 Oct	National Day *Nationalfeiertag*	A		
1 Nov	All Saints' Day *Allerheiligen*	A		
8 Dec	Immaculate Conception *Mariä Empfängnis*	A		
25/6 Dec	Christmas *Weihnachten*	A	D	CH

Emergency telephone numbers

	Austria	Germany	Switzerland
Ambulance (*Krankenwagen*)	144	112	117
Fire (*Feuerwehr*)	122	112	118
Police (*Polizei*)	133	110	117

WORDLIST

Numbers, days, seasons are given on pages 131–3.
Food is on page 155.

A

a ein/eine
about (number) ungefähr
    (time) gegen
above über
to accept nehmen
accident der Unfall
accommodation die
    Unterkunft
account das Konto
it aches es tut weh
across über
adaptor der
    Zwischenstecker
address die Adresse
admission der Eintritt
adult der/die Erwachsene
after nach
afternoon der Nachmittag
again nochmal
... ago vor ...
air conditioning die
    Klimaanlage
airline die Fluglinie
by airmail per Luftpost
airport der Flughafen
all (of them) alle
allergic to allergisch gegen
already schon
also auch
always immer
ambulance der
    Krankenwagen
America Amerika
American amerikanisch
and und
animal das Tier
ankle der Knöchel
another (more) noch ein
to answer antworten

antibiotic das Antibiotikum
antiseptic cream die
    Wundsalbe
any (pl) einige
    any more noch mehr
    any others andere
apartment die Wohnung
appointment der Termin,
    die Verabredung
arm der Arm
arrival die Ankunft
to arrive ankommen
art die Kunst
    art gallery die
    Kunstgalerie
ashtray der Aschenbecher
to ask fragen
    to ask for bitten um
aspirin das Aspirin
asthma das Asthma
at (place) an
    (time) um
    (someone's) bei
aunt die Tante
Australia Australien
Austria Österreich
automatic automatisch

B

baby das Baby
    baby food die
    Babynahrung
    babysitter der (die)
    Babysitter(-in)
back (body) der Rücken
    (direction) zurück
    at the back hinten
backpack der Rucksack

bad schlecht
bag die Tasche
baker's die Bäckerei
balcony der Balkon
ball der Ball
ballet das Ballett
bandage der Verband
bank die Bank
    bank note der
        (Geld)schein
bath das Bad
to have a bath ein Bad
        nehmen
bathroom das Badezimmer
battery die Batterie
beach der Strand
beard der Bart
beautiful schön
bed das Bett
    bed linen die Bettwäsche
beer das Bier
    beer-mug der Bierkrug
before vor
to begin beginnen
beginner der Anfänger
behind hinter
Belgium Belgien
below unter
belt der Gürtel
best beste
better besser
between zwischen
bicycle das Fahrrad
big groß
bill die Rechnung
birthday der Geburtstag
biscuit der Keks
bite der Biß
bitter bitter
black schwarz
blanket die Decke
to bleed bluten
blister die Blase
blood das Blut
    blood pressure der
        Blutdruck
blouse die Bluse
blue blau
boat das Schiff, das Boot
body der Körper
bone der Knochen
bonnet (car) die
        Motorhaube

book das Buch
to book reservieren
booking die Reservierung
    booking office der
        Reservierungsschalter
boot (car) der Kofferraum
    (shoe) der Stiefel
border die Grenze
boring langweilig
to borrow leihen
both beide
bottle die Flasche
    bottle-opener der
        Flaschenöffner
box die Schachtel
boy der Junge
boy-friend der Freund
bra der Büstenhalter (BH)
bracelet das Armband
to brake bremsen
brakes die Bremsen
brandy der Weinbrand
bread das Brot
to break brechen
breakdown die Panne
    breakdown truck der
        Abschleppwagen
breakfast das Frühstück
breast die Brust
to breathe atmen
bridge die Brücke
to bring bringen
British (adj) britisch
broken (bone) gebrochen
    (doesn't work)
        kaputt
brother der Bruder
brown braun
bruise die Quetschung
building das Gebäude
burn (injury) die
        Brandwunde
to burn brennen
bus der Bus
    bus station der
        Busbahnhof
business das Geschäft
    on ... geschäftlich
but aber
butane gas das Butangas
butcher's die Fleischerei/
        Metzgerei
butter die Butter

button der Knopf
to buy kaufen
by (author, maker) von
  (time) bis
  (= next to) neben

C

café das Café
cake der Kuchen
calculator der Rechner
call (= summon) rufen
  (= phone) anrufen
calm ruhig
camera der Fotoapparat
to camp zelten
camping equipment die
  Campingausrüstung
campsite der Campingplatz
can (= able to) können
  (of food) die Dose
Canada Kanada
to cancel annullieren
car das Auto/der Wagen
  car park der Parkplatz
caravan der Wohnwagen
carriage (railway) der
  Wagen
cash bar, das Bargeld
  cash desk die Kasse
to cash einlösen
cassette die Kassette
  cassette recorder der
    Kassettenrecorder
castle das Schloß, die Burg
cathedral der Dom, die
  Kathedrale
cave die Höhle
cellar der Keller
centre die Mitte
chain die Kette
chair der Stuhl
change das Kleingeld
to change
  (alter) ändern
  (money) wechseln
  (trains) umsteigen
charge die Gebühr/der Tarif
cheap billig
to check kontrollieren
  to check in einchecken
  to check out abreisen
checkout (shop) die Kasse

checkup (medical) die
  Untersuchung
cheers! Prost!
cheese der Käse
chemist die Apotheke/
  Drogerie
cheque der Scheck
  cheque book das
    Scheckbuch
  cheque card die
    Scheckkarte
chest die Brust
child das Kind
chips (GB) Pommes frites
chips (US) Chips
chocolate die Schokolade
chocolates (individual)
  Pralinen
to choose wählen
Christian name der
  Vorname
church die Kirche
cider der Apfelwein
cigar die Zigarre
cigarette die Zigarette
  cigarette lighter das
    Feuerzeug
cinema das Kino
circle (theatre) der Rang
city die Stadt
class die Klasse
clean sauber
to clean reinigen
clear klar
cloakroom die Garderobe
clock die Uhr
to close schließen
closed geschlossen
cloth der Stoff
clothes die Kleider
cloud die Wolke
clutch (car) die Kupplung
coach der Bus
coat der Mantel
coathanger der
  Kleiderbügel
coffee der Kaffee
coin die Münze
cold (illness) die Erkältung
  (adj) kalt
colour die Farbe
comb der Kamm
to come kommen

comfortable bequem
complicated kompliziert
concert das Konzert
  concert hall die
    Konzerthalle
conference die Konferenz
  conference centre die
    Kongreßhalle
to confirm bestätigen
congratulations! herzlichen
  Glückwunsch!
connection (transport) der
  Anschluß
constipation die
  Verstopfung
contact lens die
  Kontaktlinse
to contain enthalten
contraceptive das
  Verhütungsmittel
contract der Vertrag
to cook kochen
cool box die Kühltasche
corkscrew der
  Korkenzieher
to cost kosten
cot (child's) das Kinderbett
cotton die Baumwolle
  cotton wool die Watte
cough der Husten
country das Land
cousin der (die) Cousin(e)
cramp der Krampf
cream (from milk) die
  Sahne
credit card die Kreditkarte
credit note die Gutschrift
crisps Chips
to cross überqueren
cross-country skiing der
  Langlauf
crossroads die Kreuzung
cup die Tasse
cupboard der Schrank
currency die Währung
current (electric, water) der
  Strom
curtain der Vorhang
customs die
  Zollabfertigung
to cut schneiden
cut (= wound) die
  Schnittwunde

cycling das Radfahren

D

to dance tanzen
dangerous gefährlich
dark dunkel
daughter die Tochter
day der Tag
dead tot
to decide beschließen,
  wählen
deck chair der Liegestuhl
to declare (customs)
  verzollen
deep tief
delay die Verspätung
delicatessen das
  Delikatessengeschäft
to deliver liefern
Denmark Dänemark
dentist der Zahnarzt
denture das Gebiß
deodorant der Deodorant
department die Abteilung
  department store das
    Warenhaus
departure die Abfahrt, der
  Abflug
to leave a deposit eine
  Sicherheit hinterlegen
dessert der Nachtisch
detour (road) die Umleitung
diabetic der (die)
  Diabetiker(in)
dialling code die Vorwahl
diamond der Diamant
diaper die Windel
diarrhoea der Durchfall
diesel das Diesel
different (other) andere
  (various) verschiedene
difficult schwierig
dining car die Speisewagen
dining room (hotel) der
  Speisesaal
dinner (= evening meal)
  das Abendessen
direct direkt
  to direct (to) den Weg
    zeigen
direction die Richtung
dirty schmutzig

disabled person der/die Behinderte
disco die Disko
to dislocate verrenken
dissatisfied unzufrieden
divorced geschieden
dizzy schwindlig
to do machen
doctor der Arzt
doll die Puppe
door die Tür
dormitory der Schlafraum
double room das Doppelzimmer
down hinunter
downhill skiing der Abfahrtslauf
downstairs unten
dress das Kleid
drink das Getränk
to drink trinken
drinking water das Trinkwasser
to drip (tap) tropfen
to drive fahren
driver der Fahrer
driving licence der Führerschein
drugstore die Drogerie
dry trocken
dry cleaners die chemische Reinigung
duty-free zollfrei

E

each jeder/jede/jedes
ear das Ohr
early früh
east Ost
East Germany die DDR
easy leicht
to eat essen
electric(al) elektrisch
electricity der Stromanschluß
elevator der Fahrstuhl
embarrassing peinlich
emergency der Notfall
empty leer
end das Ende
to end enden
engaged (in use) besetzt

engine (car) der Motor
England England
English (adj) englisch
enjoyable angenehm
enough genug
entrance der Eingang
entrance fee der Eintritt
envelope der Umschlag
equipment die Ausrüstung
eraser der Radiergummi
escalator die Rolltreppe
especially besonders
Europe Europa
evening der Abend
evening meal das Abendessen
every/everyone jeder/jede/jedes
everything alles
everywhere überall
exact(ly) genau
for example zum Beispiel
except (for) außer
to exchange umtauschen
exchange rate der Wechselkurs
excursion der Ausflug
exhaust pipe der Auspuff
exhibition die Ausstellung
exit (building) der Ausgang **(motorway)** die Ausfahrt
to expect erwarten
expensive teuer
to explain erklären
extra zusätzlich
eye das Auge

F

face das Gesicht
factory die Fabrik
faint (feeling) schwach
to fall fallen
family die Familie
famous berühmt
fan belt der Keilriemen
far weit
fare der Fahrpreis
farm fer Bauernhof
fashionable modisch
fast schnell
fat dick

141

father der Vater
favourite Lieblings-
to fax ein Telefax schicken
I feel ... (ill/happy) ich
    fühle mich ...
ferry die Fähre
to fetch holen
fever das Fieber
a few ein paar
fiancé(e) der (die) Verlobte
field das Feld
to fill füllen
   to fill in (form) ausfüllen
filling (tooth) die Plombe
filling station die Tankstelle
film der Film
to find finden
fine (money) die Geldstrafe
  (OK) gut/OK
finger der Finger
fire das Feuer, der Brand
  fire brigade die
    Feuerwehr
firm (company) die Firma
first-aid kit der
  Verbandkasten
fish der Fisch
fishing das Angeln
  fishing permit der
    Angelschein
  fishing tackle das
    Angelzeug
to fit passen
fizzy mit Kohlensäure
flashgun (photo) der Blitz
flat (battery) leer
  (apartment) die
    Wohnung
  (shape) flach
flight der Flug
  flight number die
    Flugnummer
floor (storey) der Stock
florist das Blumengeschäft
flower die Blume
flu die Grippe
to fly fliegen
fog der Nebel
food das Essen
  food poisoning die
    Lebensmittelvergiftung
foot der Fuß
  on foot zu Fuß

football der Fußball
footpath der Fußweg
for für
  (+ past time) seit
  (+ future time) für
foreigner der (die)
  Ausländer(in)
forest der Wald
to forget vergessen
fork die Gabel
form das Formular
fortnight zwei Wochen
forwarding address die
  Nachsendeadresse
fountain der Brunnen
fountain pen der Füller
fracture der Bruch
frame (glasses) das Gestell
France Frankreich
free kostenlos
to freeze frieren
french (adj) französisch
french fries die Pommes
  frites
fresh frisch
friend der (die) Freund(in)
friendly freundlich
from von, aus
front vorne, Vorder-
fruit das Obst
fruit-juice der Fruchtsaft
full voll
  I'm full Ich bin satt
  full board die
    Vollpension
  full up (hotel) belegt
funny komisch
furniture die Möbel
fuse die Sicherung

G

game (meat) das Wild
  (play) das Spiel
garage (repairs) die
  Reparaturwerkstatt
garden der Garten
gas das Gas
gasoline das Benzin
gate das Tor
gear box das Getriebe
genuine echt
German (adj) deutsch

Germany Deutschland
to get (become) werden
(fetch) holen
(obtain) bekommen
to get on (bus) einsteigen
to get off (bus) aussteigen
to get to kommen nach/zu
to get to know
kennenlernen
to get up aufstehen
gin der Gin
girl das Mädchen
girl-friend die Freundin
to give geben
glass das Glas
glasses die Brille
gloves die Handschuhe
glue der Klebstoff
to go gehen, fahren
to go out ausgehen
gold das Gold
gold-plated vergoldet
golf das Golf
golf course der Golfplatz
good gut
good-bye (in person) Auf
Wiedersehen
(phone) Auf
Wiederhören
grass das Gras
greasy fettig
Great Britain
Großbritannien
green grün
greengrocer's die
Gemüsehandlung
grey grau
grocer's das
Lebensmittelgeschäft
ground floor das
Erdgeschoß
group die Gruppe
guarantee die Garantie
guide der Führer/die
Führerin
guide book der Reiseführer
guided tour die Führung
gum (teeth) der Zahnfleisch

H

hair die Haare
hairbrush die Haarbürste

hairdresser's der Friseur
hairdryer der
Haartrockner
half die Hälfte, halb
half board die
Halbpension
half price zum halben
Preis
hand die Hand
handbag die Handtasche
handkerchief das
Taschentuch
hand luggage das
Handgepäck
handsome schön
happy glücklich
harbour der Hafen
hard (surface) hart
hat der Hut
to have haben
hay fever der Heuschnupfen
he er
head der Kopf
headache Kopfschmerzen
headlights die
Scheinwerfer
healthy gesund
to hear hören
heart das Herz
heart attack der
Herzinfarkt
heating die Heizung
heavy schwer
heel (shoe) der Absatz
hello! hallo!
to help helfen
help! hilfe!
her ihr
here hier
high hoch
hill der Berg, der Hügel
to hire mieten
his/him sein/ihn
history die Geschichte
to hitchhike trampen
to hold halten
hole das Loch
holidays die Ferien/der
Urlaub
home address der Wohnort
horse das Pferd
horse-riding das
Pferdereiten

hospital das Krankenhaus
hot heiß
hotel das Hotel
hour die Stunde
how? wie?
  how about...? wie wäre
    es mit...?
  how far? wie weit?
  how many? wie viele?
  how much? wieviel?
hunger der Hunger
  I'm hungry ich habe
    Hunger
hurry up! beeilen Sie sich!
it hurts es tut weh
husband der Mann

I

I ich
ice das Eis
  ice-cream das Eis
  ice-lolly das Eis am Stiel
  ice-rink das Eisstadion
  ice-skating das Eislaufen
ill krank
immediate(ly) sofort
important wichtig
impossible unmöglich
in in
including inbegriffen
indigestion die
    Magenverstimmung
infection die Infektion
information die Auskunft
  information office das
    Informationsbüro
injection die Spritze
injured verletzt
injury die Verletzung
insect bite der Insektenstich
insect repellent der
    Insektenschutz
inside drinnen
instead (of that) statt
    (dessen)
insurance die Versicherung
interesting interessant
international international
interpreter der (die)
    Dolmetscher(in)
to introduce vorstellen
to invite einladen

invitation die Einladung
Ireland Irland
to iron bügeln
island die Insel
it es
Italian (adj) italienisch
Italy Italien

J

jacket die Jacke
jam die Marmelade
to jam (get stuck) klemmen
jar das Glas
jeans die Jeans
jeweller's der Juwelier
jewellery der Schmuck
to go jogging joggen gehen
journey die Reise
juice der Saft
just (only) nur

K

to keep behalten
key der Schlüssel
kilo das Kilo
kilometre der Kilometer
kind nett, freundlich
kitchen die Küche
knee das Knie
knife das Messer
to knock klopfen
to know (about) wissen
    (person, place) kennen

L

lace die Spitze
lady die Dame/die Frau
lake der See
landscape die Landschaft
large groß
last letzte
to last dauern
late spät
to laugh lachen
launderette der Waschsalon
laxative das Abführmittel
lead-free bleifrei
to learn lernen
at least mindestens
leather das Leder
to leave (something) lassen

144

(depart) abfahren
to leave luggage das Gepäck
  einstellen
left linke
to the left links
leg das Bein
lemonade die Limonade
less weniger
letter der Brief
library die Bibliothek
licence die Erlaubnis
  (driving) der
    Führerschein
to lie down sich hinlegen
life belt der Rettungsring
lift der Fahrstuhl
light (colour) hell
  (not heavy) leicht
  (lamp) die Lampe
  light bulb die Birne
like (similar) ähnlich
  I like . . . . . . gefällt mir
line die Linie
lip die Lippe
lipsalve der Lippensalb
lipstick der Lippenstift
liqueur der Likör
to listen hören
litre der Liter
little klein
(a) little ein wenig
to live wohnen
loaf (of bread) das Brot
local aus der Gegend
long lang
to look sehen
  to look for suchen
to have a look (in shop) sich
  umsehen
loose (clothes) weit
  (screw) locker
to lose verlieren
to get lost sich verirren
lost property office das
  Fundbüro
a lot (of) viel/viele
to love lieben
lovely schön
low niedrig
luggage das Gepäck
  luggage trolley der
    Kofferkuli
lunch das Mittagessen

M

machine die Maschine
made of aus
magazine die Illustrierte
mail die Post
main Haupt-
to make machen
man der Mann
manager der Manager
many viele
map die Karte
market der Markt
married verheiratet
mass (church) die Messe
match (game) der
  Wettkampf
  (lighter) das
    Streichholz
mattress die Matratze
material der Stoff
may I? kann ich?
meal das Essen
to measure Maß nehmen
meat das Fleisch
mechanic der Mechaniker
medical ärztlich
  medical certificate der
    Krankenschein
  medical insurance die
    Krankenkasse
medicine das Medikament
medium-sized mittelgroß
to meet treffen
member das Mitglied
to mend flicken
menu die Speisekarte
message die Nachricht
middle die Mitte
migraine die Migräne
milk die Milch
mineral water das
  Mineralwasser
minute die Minute
mirror der Spiegel
to miss (train) verpassen
mistake der Fehler
mixed gemischt
modern modern
moment der Augenblick
money das Geld
month der Monat
more mehr

morning der Morgen
most(ly) meist(ens)
mother die Mutter
motorbike das Motorrad
motor boat das Motorboot
motorway die Autobahn
mountain der Berg
mountaineering das
    Bergsteigen
moustache der Schnurrbart
mouth der Mund
to move bewegen
movies das Kino
Mr Herr
Mrs/Ms Frau
much viel
mug der Becher
muscle der Muskel
museum das Museum
music die Musik
must müssen
my mein

N

nail der Nagel
  nail clippers die
      Nagelzange
  nail polish der Nagellack
  nail polish remover der
      Nagellackentferner
name der Name
napkin die Serviette
nappy die Windel
narrow eng
nationality die Nationalität
near nah
nearest nächste
neck der Hals
to need brauchen
needle die Nadel
Netherlands die
    Niederlande
never nie
new neu
New Zealand Neuseeland
newsagent's der
    Zeitungshändler
newspaper die Zeitung
next nächste
  next time nächstes Mal
  next to neben
nice (thing) nett/schön

(person) sympathisch
night die Nacht
  night club das
      Nachtlokal
no nein
noisy laut
non-alcoholic alkoholfrei
none keine
non-smoker der
    Nichtraucher
normally normalerweise
north Nord
Norway Norwegen
nose die Nase
nosebleed das Nasenbluten
not nicht
  not yet noch nicht
nothing nichts
now jetzt
number (of house, etc) die
    Nummer
      (quantity) der Zahl
  number plate das
      Nummernschild
nurse die Krankenschwester
nursery slopes der
    Anfängerhügel

O

occupied besetzt
office das Büro
oil das Öl
old alt
on an, auf
once einmal
one-way street die
    Einbahnstraße
one-way (ticket) einfach
only nur
open offen
to open öffnen
opening times (shops,
    museums) Öffnungs-
    zeiten
      (business) Geschäfts-
      zeiten
opera die Oper
opposite gegenüber
optician der Optiker
or oder
orchestra das Orchester
to order bestellen

other andere
our unser
out of order außer Betrieb
outside draußen
over über
to overheat heißlaufen

P

to pack einpacken
packet die Schachtel
page die Seite
pain der Schmerz
painkiller das Schmerzmittel
paint die Farbe
to paint malen
painting das Bild
pair das Paar
palace der Palast
pants (GB) die Unterhose
  (US) die Hose
paper das Papier
paperback das Taschenbuch
parcel das Paket
pardon? wie bitte?
parents die Eltern
park der Park
to park parken
parking disc die Parkscheibe
parking meter die Parkuhr
party die Party
pass (bus) die Mehrfahrkarte
  (mountain) der Paß
passenger der Fahrgast/der Reisende
passport der Paß
  passport photo das Paßbild
pastry das Gebäck
patient der (die) Patient(in)
to pay (be)zahlen
pedestrian der Fußgänger
pen (ball-point) der Kuli
  (fountain) der Füller
pencil der Bleistift
  pencil sharpener der Bleistiftspitzer
penicillin das Penizillin

pensioner der (die) Rentner(in)
people die Leute
per pro
performance die Aufführung
perfume das Parfüm
period pains Menstruations-schmerzen
perm die Dauerwelle
permit die Genehmigung
perhaps vielleicht
personal persönlich
petrol das Benzin
  petrol station die Tankstelle
phone das Telefon
to phone anrufen
phone box die Telefonzelle
phone call der Anruf/das Gespräch
phone number die Telefonnummer
photo das Foto
photocopy die Fotokopie
to photograph fotografieren
to pick someone up abholen
picnic das Picknick
picture das Bild
piece das Stück
pill die Pille, die Tablette
pin die Nadel
pink rosa
pipe die Pfeife
place der Ort
place of birth der Geburtsort
places of interest die Sehenswürdigkeiten
plan der Plan
to plan planen
plane das Flugzeug
plaster (sticking) das Pflaster
plastic das Plastik
  plastic bag die Plastiktüte
plate der Teller
platform (station) der Bahnsteig/das Gleis
play (theatre) das Stück
to play spielen
playground der Spielplatz

playing cards die Spielkarten
please bitte
plug (electric) der Stecker
  (water) der Stöpsel
pocket die Tasche
to point zeigen
poison das Gift
poisoning die Vergiftung
police die Polizei
  police station das Polizeirevier
  police (wo)man der Polizist(in)
port der Hafen
portable tragbar
porter der Gepäckträger
portion die Portion
possibly vielleicht
post die Post
to post aufgeben
post box der Briefkasten
post card die Postkarte, die Ansichtskarte
post office die Post
pound (money/weight) das Pfund
powder der Puder
pregnant schwanger
prescription das Rezept
present das Geschenk
pretty hübsch
price der Preis
private privat
probably wahrscheinlich
problem das Problem
processing (film) die Entwicklung
profession der Beruf
programme das Programm
pub das Lokal/die Wirtschaft
public holiday der Feiertag
to pull ziehen
pullover der Pullover
pump die Pumpe
to pump up aufpumpen
puncture das Loch
punctual pünktlich
pure rein
purse das Portemonnaie
to push (button) drücken
  (car) schieben

to put stellen
pyjamas der Schlafanzug

Q

quality die Qualität
question die Frage
to queue Schlange stehen
quick(ly) schnell
quiet ruhig

R

radiator (car) der Kühler
radio das Radio
by rail mit der Bahn
railway station der Bahnhof
to rain regnen
rash (medical) der Ausschlag
razor der Rasierapparat
to read lesen
ready fertig
real echt
rear hinten/Hinter-
receipt die Quittung
receive bekommen
receptionist der Empfangschef
to recommend empfehlen
record die Schallplatte
red rot
refill (pen) die Ersatzmine
to give a refund das Geld zurückgeben
region die Gegend
registration form das Anmeldeformular
to rent mieten
repair die Reparatur
to repair reparieren
repair kit das Flickzeug
to repeat wiederholen
to reserve reservieren
restaurant das Restaurant/die Gaststätte
return ticket hin und zurück
to return (give back) zurückgeben
  (travel back) zurückfahren
reverse charge call das R-Gespräch
to the right rechts

right (correct) richtig
ring der Ring
to ring (doorbell) klingeln
    (phone someone)
    anrufen
ripe reif
river der Fluß
road die Straße
  road map die
    Straßenkarte
  road sign das
    Verkehrsschild
romantic romantisch
room das Zimmer
    (space) der Platz
  room service der
    Zimmerservice
rope das Seil
round rund
route die Strecke
rubber (eraser) der
    Radiergummi
    (material) der
    Gummi
rucksack der Rucksack
ruin der Ruine
ruler (measure) das Lineal
to run laufen

S

safe ungefährlich
    (strongbox) der Safe
safety pin die
    Sicherheitsnadel
to sail segeln
sale der Schlußverkauf
for sale zu verkaufen
sanitary towel die
    Damenbinde
saucepan der Kochtopf
sausage die Wurst
scarf das Halstuch, der
    Schal
scheduled planmäßig
school die Schule
science die
    Naturwissenschaften
scissors die Schere
Scotland Schottland
screwdriver der
    Schraubenzieher
sea die See

seat der Platz
  seat belt der
    Sicherheitsgurt
second (time) die Sekunde
second-hand gebraucht,
    antiquarisch
secretary der (die)
    Sekretär(in)
to see sehen
self-service Selbstbedienung
    (SB)
to sell verkaufen
to send schicken
separate(ly) getrennt
service (church) das
    Gottesdienst
    (restaurant) die
    Bedienung
services (motorway) die
    Raststätte
serviette die Serviette
to sew nähen
shampoo das Shampoo
sharp scharf
to shave rasieren
shaver der Rasierapparat
shaving cream die
    Rasiercreme
she sie
ship das Schiff
shirt das Hemd
shoe der Schuh
  shoelace der
    Schnürsenkel
  shoe polish die
    Schuhcreme
  shoe repairer's der
    Schuhmacher
  shoeshop das
    Schuhgeschäft
shop das Geschäft, der
    Laden
to go shopping einkaufen
    gehen
shop window das
    Schaufenster
shopping centre das
    Einkaufszentrum
short kurz
shorts die Shorts
shoulder die Schulter
to show zeigen
shower die Dusche   149

shut geschlossen
to shut schließen
shutter (window) der Fensterladen
sick (ill) krank
to be sick spucken
sickness (illness) die Krankheit
side die Seite
sightseeing die Besichtigung
sign das Schild
to sign unterschreiben
signature die Unterschrift
silk die Seide
silver das Silber
silver-plated versilbert
simple einfach
since seit
to sing singen
single (ticket) einfach (unmarried) ledig
single room das Einzelzimmer
sister die Schwester
size (clothes) die Größe (shoes) die Nummer
skates Schlittschuhe
to skate eislaufen
skating rink die Eisbahn
skis Skier
to ski skilaufen
ski-boot der Skischuh
ski-lift der Skilift
skin die Haut
skirt der Rock
sky der Himmel
to sleep schlafen
sleeping bag der Schlafsack
sleeping car der Schlafwagen
sleeve der Ärmel
slice die Scheibe
slide (photo) das Dia
slippers Hausschuhe
slow(ly) langsam
small klein
to smoke rauchen
smoker der Raucher
snack der Imbiß
snow der Schnee
to snow schneien
soap die Seife
sock die Socke

socket (electric) die Steckdose
soft weich
soft drink ein alkoholfreies Getränk
sole (shoe) die Sohle
some (pl) einige
someone jemand
something (else) etwas (anderes)
sometimes manchmal
son der Sohn
song das Lied/der Song
soon bald
I'm sorry Entschuldigung
sour sauer
south Süd
souvenir das Andenken
Spain Spanien
Spanish spanisch
spare part das Ersatzteil
spare tyre der Ersatzreifen
spark plug die Zündkerze
to speak sprechen
special offer das Sonderangebot
speciality die Spezialität
spectator die Zuschauer
to spell buchstabieren
to spend ausgeben
spoon der Löffel
sport der Sport
square (shape) viereckig (in town) der Platz
stadium das Stadion
stain der Fleck
stairs die Treppe
stalls (theatre) das Parkett
stamp (postage) die Briefmarke
to start beginnen (car) anspringen
station (rail) der Bahnhof (underground) die Station
stationer's das Schreibwarengeschäft
to stay (on holiday) wohnen (remain) bleiben
to steal stehlen
sting der Stich
stolen gestohlen
stomach der Magen

stop (bus) die Haltestelle
stop! halt!
to stop (halt) halten
    (doing something)
    aufhören
store (shop) der Laden/das
    Geschäft
storm das Unwetter
straight direkt/gerade
straight on geradeaus
street die Straße
  street map der Stadtplan
string der Bindfaden
strong stark
student der (die) Student(in)
to study studieren
subway (US) die U-bahn
suede das Wildleder
sugar der Zucker
suit (clothes) der Anzug
suitcase der Koffer
sun die Sonne
to sunbathe in der Sonne
    liegen
sunburn der Sonnenbrand
sunglasses die Sonnenbrille
sunshade der Sonnenschirm
sun-tan cream die
    Sonnencreme
supermarket der
    Supermarkt
supper (evening meal) das
    Abendessen
surcharge der Zuschlag
surname der Nachname
to swallow schlucken
Sweden Schweden
sweet (flavour) süß
sweets Bonbons
to swim schwimmen
swimming pool das
    Schwimmbad
  (indoor) das Hallenbad
  (outdoor) das Freibad
swimming trunks die
    Badehose
swimsuit der Badeanzug
Swiss (adj) schweizerisch
Switzerland die Schweiz
swollen geschwollen
synagogue die Synagoge

T

table der Tisch
to take nehmen
    (time) dauern
take-away (food) zum
    Mitnehmen
taken (occupied) besetzt
tall groß
tampon der Tampon
tap der Hahn
taxi das Taxi
  taxi rank der Taxistand
tea der Tee
  tea bag der Teebeutel
  teaspoon der Teelöffel
technology die Technik
television der Fernseher
to tell sagen
temperature die
    Temperatur
    (= fever) das Fieber
temporary provisorisch
tent das Zelt
  tent peg der Hering
  tent pole die Zeltstange
tennis das Tennis
  tennis court der
    Tennisplatz
  tennis racket der
    Tennisschläger
terminus die Endstation
terrible schrecklich
than als
thank you danke
that (one) der/die/das
the der/die/das
theatre das Theater
their ihr
then dann
there dort
there is/there are es gibt
thermometer das
    Thermometer
these diese
they sie
thick dick
thief der Dieb
thin dünn
to think (believe)
    glauben
I'm thirsty ich habe Durst
this (one) dieser/diese/dieses 151

thread der Faden
throat der Hals
  throat pastille die
    Halspastille
through durch
thumb der Daumen
thunderstorm das Gewitter
ticket (bus) der Fahrschein
    (plane) die Flugkarte
    (rail) die Fahrkarte
    (entrance) die
      (Eintritts) Karte
    (dry cleaner's) der
      Zettel
ticket office der
    Fahrkartenschalter
tide (high) die Flut
    (low) die Ebbe
tie die Krawatte
tight eng
tights die Strumpfhose
till die Kasse
time (measure) die Zeit
    (occasion) das Mal
    next time nächstes Mal
on time pünktlich
tin (can) die Dose
tin-opener der Dosenöffner
tire (US) der Reifen
tired müde
tissues Papiertücher
to (town, country) nach
    (building, road) zu
tobacco der Tabak
tobacconist's der
    Tabakladen
today heute
toe die Zehe
together zusammen
toilet die Toilette
  toilet paper das
    Toilettenpapier
toiletries Toilettenartikel
toll die Gebühr, die Maut
tomorrow morgen
  tomorrow morning
    morgen früh
tongue die Zunge
tonight heute abend
too (much) zu
    (also) auch
tooth der Zahn
  toothache die
    Zahnschmerzen
toothbrush die
    Zahnbürste
toothpaste die Zahnpasta
torch die Taschenlampe
to touch berühren
tour die Rundfahrt, der
    Rundgang
tourist office das
    Fremdenverkehrsbüro
to tow abschleppen
towards gegen
towel das Handtuch
tower der Turm
town die Stadt
  town centre die
    Innenstadt
toy das Spielzeug
traffic (road) der Verkehr
  traffic jam der Stau
  traffic light die Ampel
trailer der Anhänger, der
    Wohnwagen (US)
train der Zug
by train mit der Bahn
transfer (bank) die
    Überweisung
to translate übersetzen
to travel reisen
  travel agent das
    Reisebüro
  travel sickness die
    Reisekrankheit
traveller's cheque der
    Reisescheck
tree der Baum
trip (excursion) der Ausflug
trousers die Hose
to try (attempt) versuchen
    (sample) probieren
  to try on anprobieren
tube die Tube
twice zweimal
twin beds zwei Einzelbetten
to type tippen
typewriter die
    Schreibmaschine
tyre der Reifen

U

umbrella der Regenschirm
uncle der Onkel

unconscious bewußtlos
under unter
underground (railway) die U-bahn
underpants die Unterhose
to understand verstehen
United States die Vereinigten Staaten
university die Universität
until bis
up hinauf
upset stomach die Magenverstimmung
upstairs oben
urgent dringend
to use benutzen
useful nützlich

V

vacancy ein freies Zimmer
'no vacancies' 'belegt'
vacant frei
vacation die Ferien, der Urlaub
valley das Tal
VAT MwSt (Mehrwertsteuer)
vegetables das Gemüse
vegetarian vegetarisch
very sehr
view die Aussicht
village das Dorf
vineyard der Weinberg
visit der Besuch
to visit besuchen
voltage die (Strom)Spannung
to vomit spucken, sich übergeben

W

to wait warten
waiter der Kellner/Herr Ober!
waiting room der Wartesaal
waitress die Kellnerin/ Bedienung!
Wales Wales
to go for a walk einen Spaziergang machen
to walk zu Fuß gehen

walking (hiking) das Wandern
wallet die Brieftasche
to want wollen
to wash waschen
wash basin das Waschbecken
washing powder das Waschpulver
washing-up liquid das Spülmittel
watch (clock) die Armbanduhr
to watch sehen
water das Wasser
waterfall der Wasserfall
waterproof wasserdicht
waterskiing das Wasserskilaufen
we wir
to wear tragen
weather das Wetter
weather forecast der Wetterbericht
week die Woche
weekend das Wochenende
well (feeling) gut
(healthy) wohl
(water) der Brunnen
west West
West Germany die Bundesrepublik
what? was?
wheel das Rad
wheelchair der Rollstuhl
where? wo?
when? wann?
which? welcher/welche/ welches?
white weiß
who? wer?
whole ganz
why? warum?
wide breit
wife die Frau
wind der Wind
window das Fenster
windscreen die Windschutzscheibe
windscreen wiper der Scheibenwischer
windsurfing das Windsurfen

wine der Wein
with mit
without ohne
woman die Dame/die Frau
wonderful wunderbar
wood (forest) der Wald
    (material) das Holz
wool die Wolle
word das Wort
to work (job) arbeiten
    (function) funktionier-
    en
worse schlechter
to wrap einpacken
to write schreiben
writing paper das
    Schreibpapier
wrong falsch

X

to X-ray röntgen

Y

year das Jahr
yellow gelb
yes ja
yesterday gestern
yet noch
you du (friend)/Sie (polite)
young jung
your dein (friend)/Ihr
    (polite)
youth hostel die
    Jugendherberge

Z

zip der Reißverschluß
zoo der Zoo

What's on the menu?

- The immense variety of German regional cookery makes it impossible to do much more here than to list the main vocabulary to be found on menus. Most menus explain what goes into each dish. The list is divided into:
  - Savoury pages 155–9.
  - Sweet pages 159–60.

Savoury

Artischocken *aartishoken*	artichokes	**Brokkoli** *brokolee*	broccoli
Auberginen *ohberjeenen*	aubergines	**Champignons** *shampinyongs*	mushrooms
Auflauf *owflowf*	casserole	**Dorsch** *dorsh*	cod
Austern *owstern*	oysters	**Eier** *I-er*	eggs
Back- *bak-*	roasted	**mit Einlage** *mit ynlaager*	egg, vegetables, etc, added to a clear soup
Beilagen *by-laagen*	side-dish (vegetable or salad)		
Blumenkohl *bloomen-kohl*	cauliflower	**Eintopf** *yntopf*	stew
Bockwurst *bokvoorst*	frankfurter	**englisch** *ennglish*	rare (meat)
Bohnen *bohnen*	beans	**Ente** *enter*	duck
grüne *grewner*	green (French)	**Erbsen** *airbzen*	peas
weiße *vysser*	white (haricot)	**Essig** *essig*	vinegar
Brat- *braat*	roasted	**Filet** *filai*	fillet
Bratwurst *braatvoorst*	fried sausage	**Fleischpastete** *flysh-pastaiter*	pâté

155

Forelle *foreller*	trout	**hausgemacht** *hows-germakht*	home-made
Gans *gans*	goose	**Hering** *Hairing*	herring
Garnelen *gaarnailen*	prawns	**Huhn** *hoon*	chicken
gebacken *gerbaken*	baked	**Hühnerbrühe** *hewnerbrewer*	chicken broth
gebraten *gerbraaten*	roasted	**Hummer** *hoomer*	lobster
gedämpft *gerdempft*	steamed	**Ingwer** *ingver*	ginger
Geflügel *gerflewgel*	poultry	**Jäger-** *yaiger*	with a spicy sauce
gefüllt *gerfewlt*	stuffed	**Kabeljau** *kaabelyow*	cod
gegrillt *gergrillt*	grilled	**Kalb (-fleisch)** *kalp (-flysh)*	veal
gehackt *gerhakt*	chopped/minced	**Kalte Platte** *kalter platter*	selection of cold meats
gekocht *gerkokht*	cooked/boiled	**Kaninchen** *kaneenkhen*	rabbit
geräuchert *geroykhert*	smoked	**Karotten** *karoten*	carrots
gewürzt *gervewrtst*	flavoured with spices	**Kartoffeln** *kaartoffeln*	potatoes
grüner Salat *grewner zalaat*	green salad	**Kartoffelbrei** *kaartofferlbr-I*	mashed potatoes
Gurken *goorken*	cucumbers/gherkins	**Klößchen** *klurskhen*	dumplings
Hackfleisch *hakflysh*	minced meat	**Knackwurst** *knakvoorst*	type of Frankfurter
Hähnchen *hainkhen*	chicken	**Knoblauch** *knohb-lowkh*	garlic
Hauptgerichte *howpt-gerikhter*	main courses	**Kohl** *kohl*	cabbage

156

Kopfsalat *kopfzalaat*	lettuce	**Nieren** *neeren*	kidneys
Kotelett *kohtelet*	chop/cutlet	**Nudeln** *noodeln*	noodles
Krabben *krabben*	shrimps/ prawns	**Oliven** *oleeven*	olives
Kräuter *kroyter*	herbs	**paniert** *paneert*	cooked in breadcrumbs
Krebs *krebz*	crab	**Paprikaschoten** *papreeka- shohten*	green peppers
Lachs *lakhs*	salmon	**Paradeiser** *paradyzer*	tomatoes
Lamm (-fleisch) *lam (-flysh)*	lamb	**Pellkartoffeln** *pell-kaartoffeln*	potatoes boiled in their jackets
Lauch *lowkh*	leek	**Pfannkuchen** *pfankookhen*	pancake
Leber *laiber*	liver	**Pfeffer** *pfeffer*	pepper
Leipziger Allerlei *lyptsiger alerl-I*	mixed vegetables	**Pilze** *piltser*	mushrooms
Linsen *linzen*	lentils	**Pommes frites** *pom frit*	chips (french fries)
Mais *mys*	sweetcorn	**Porree** *porai*	leek
Makrele *makrailer*	mackerel	**Poulet** *poolay*	chicken
Meeresfrüchte *mairesfrewkhter*	seafood	**Puter** *pooter*	turkey
zum Mitnehmen *tsoom mitnaimen*	to take away	**Radieschen** *radeeskhen*	radishes
Möhren *muren*	carrots	**Reh** *rai*	venison
Mohrrüben *mohrewben*	carrots	**Reis** *rys*	rice

Rind (-fleisch) *rint (-flysh)*	beef	**Schlachtplatte** *shlakhtplatter*	selection of cold meats and sausages
Rippchen *ripkhen*	spareribs		
Rohschinken *roh-shinken*	cured ham	**Schnitzel** *shnitzel*	escalope
Rosenkohl *rohzenkohl*	Brussels sprouts	**Scholle** *sholler*	plaice
Rostbraten *rostbraaten*	roast	**Schweine- (-fleisch)** *shvyner (-flysh)*	pork
rote Beete *rohte baite*	beetroot	**Seezunge** *zai-tsoonger*	sole
Rotkohl *rohtkohl*	red cabbage	**Semmelknödel** *zemmelknurdel*	bread dumplings
Russische Eier *roosisher I-er*	eggs/ mayonnaise	**Senf** *zenf*	mustard
Salat *zalaat*	salad	**Spargel** *shpaargel*	asparagus
Salm *zalm*	salmon	**Speck** *shpek*	bacon
Salz *zalts*	salt	**Spinat** *shpinaat*	spinach
Salzkartoffeln *zalts-kaartoffeln*	boiled potatoes	**Stangensellerie** *shtangernzeleree*	celery
Sardinen *zaardeenen*	sardines	**Strammer Max** *shtrammer max*	ham and fried egg on bread
Sauerbraten *zowerbraaten*	marinaded braised beef	**Suppe** *zooper*	soup
scharf *shaarf*	hot/highly seasoned	**süß-sauer** *zews-zower*	sweet and sour
Schaschlik *shashlik*	kebab	**Teigwaren** *tygvaaren*	pasta
Schinken *shinken*	ham	**Thunfisch** *toonfish*	tuna
		Tomaten *tomaaten*	tomatoes

Truthahn *troothaan*	turkey	**Wild** *vilt*	game/venison
vegetarisch *vegetaarish*	vegetarian	**Wurstplatte** *voorstplatter*	selection of cold sausage
Vorspeisen *fohr-shpyzen*	starters	**Würze** *vewrtser*	seasoning/spice
Weißkohl *vyskohl*	white cabbage	**Zucchini** *tsoocheeni*	courgettes
Wiener Schnitzel *veener shnitzel*	veal escalope	**Zwiebeln** *tsveebeln*	onions

Sweet

Ananas *ananas*	pineapple	**Eisbecher** *I-s-bekher*	sundae/ice cream
Apfel *apfel*	apple	**Erdbeeren** *airdbairen*	strawberries
Apfelsine *apfelzeener*	orange	**Erdnüsse** *airdnewsser*	peanuts
Aprikose *aprikohzen*	apricot	**Feigen** *fygen*	figs
Backpflaumen *bak-pflowmen*	prunes	**Gebäck** *gerbek*	cakes/pastries/biscuits
Baiser *bezai*	meringue	**Haselnüsse** *haazelnewsser*	hazelnuts
Banane *banaaner*	banana	**Himbeeren** *himbairen*	raspberries
Berliner *berleener*	jam doughnut	**Honig** *hohnig*	honey
Birne *beerner*	pear	**Johannisbeeren** *yohannisbairen*	currants
Brombeeren *brombeeren*	blackberries	**rote** *rohter*	red
Datteln *dateln*	dates	**schwarze** *shvaartser*	black

Kaffee *kafai*	coffee	**Pflaumen** *pflowmen*	plums
Käsekuchen *kaizer-kookhen*	cheesecake	**Rahm** *raam*	cream
Kirschen *keershen*	cherries	**Rhabarber** *rabaarber*	rhubarb
Kokosnuß *kohkosnoos*	coconut	**Ribisel** *reebizl*	currants
Kuchen *kookhen*	cake/gateau	**Rosinen** *rohzeenen*	raisins
Limone *limohner*	lime	**mit/ohne Sahne** *mit/ohner zaaner*	with/without cream
Mandarine *mandareener*	mandarin/tangerine	**Schlagsahne** *shlaagzaaner*	whipped cream
Mandeln *mandeln*	almonds	**Schokolade** *shokohlaader*	chocolate
Melone *melohner*	melon	**Teig** *tyg*	pastry
Mokka *moka*	coffee	**Torte** *torter*	gâteau/flan
Mus *moos*	puree	**Walnuss** *vaalnoos*	walnut
Nüsse *newsser*	nuts	**Wassermelone** *vassermelohner*	water-melon
Obst *ohbst*	fruit	**Weintrauben** *vyntrowben*	grapes
Orange *oronjer*	orange	**Zitrone** *tsitrohner*	lemon
Pampelmuse *pampelmoozer*	grapefruit	**Zucker** *tsooker*	sugar
Pfirsich *pfeerzikh*	peach	**Zwetschgen** *tsvechen*	damsons